Minolta® X-370, X-300, and Seagull DF-300

A David Hancock Tutorial Walkthrough

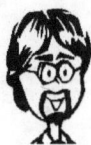

Part of The David Hancock Camera Tutorials Walkthrough Series

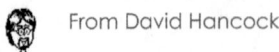 From David Hancock

Minolta® X-370

A David Hancock Tutorial Walkthrough

ALL RIGHTS RESERVED. No part of this work may be reproduced, copied, stored, transmitted, or used in any form or using electronic, graphic, or mechanical, including but not limited to recording, photocopying, scanning, digitizing, photographing, web distribution, or information networks and storage systems, except as permitted under Section 107 or 108 of the 1976 United States Copyright Act, without prior, written permission of the author.

Developed and released by 5119, LLC.

Minolta is a trademark of JMM Lee Properties, LLC.

All images in this book are created, modified, and copyrighted by David Hancock unless otherwise noted.

ISBN: 979-832378-341-0

David Hancock is a recognized and respected photography education YouTube personality. For more information about David Hancock, visit his YouTube channel:
https://www.youtube.com/c/davidhancock

© 2022-2024 David Hancock

For my wife Sulastri and her encouragement of this series.

For my YouTube subscribers and channel members whose viewership makes these books possible.

About the Author

David Hancock, also known as YouTube's Photography Professor, authors and produces camera and photography instructional videos that provide learning photographers with the basic skills needed to operate a camera. Known for his comprehensive, thorough, and well-explained camera manuals, Mr. Hancock also creates videos that teach photographers how to use specific films and lenses, and incorporate techniques into their work. This book series uses his camera manual outline to provide a written companion to his video manuals.

Mr. Hancock has more than 35 years of photography experience, more than 25 years of writing experience, and more than ten years creating YouTube content with more than 1,000 photography-education videos on his channel, and he taught college English for four years. His instruction manuals and YouTube content combine those experiences to create clear, easily followed, and readily understood guides that help photographers learn their tools quickly and focus on the important work of honing their creative vision and voice.

Highly accessible to learning photographers, Mr. Hancock welcomes questions, comments, feedback, and requests and greatly enjoys his time directly helping photographers improve their work. Mr. Hancock can be found hiking in Colorado's mountains with his wife Sulastri and little brown dog Steinbeck. If you see him, say hi.

Table of Contents

Introduction — 1

1. The Minolta X-370 Details — 3
1.1. Minolta X-370 Statistics at a Glance: 3
1.2. About the Minolta X-370 4

2. What are the Buttons? — 6
2.1. Top Controls 6
2.2. Front Controls 13
2.3. Back Controls 18
2.4. Bottom Controls 18
2.5. Film Chamber (Inside) 19

3. Basic Operation — 22
3.1. Change the Battery 22
3.2. Film Loading 23
3.3. Lens Mounting and Unmounting 27
3.4. Focusing a Lens 28

4. Flash Basics — 30

5. Reading the Light Meter — 32

6. Take a Photo — 36

7. Tips for using the Minolta X-370 — 37
7.1. Using the Light Meter Effectively 37
7.2. How to take Double Exposures 38
7.3. General Care and Use 41

8. Known Problems — 43

Acronym List

A	AUTO (Automatic, Aperture-Priority Mode)
AEL	Auto-exposure Lock
ASA	American Standards Association
B	Bulb
C-W	Center-weighted
DIN	Deutsches Institut für Normung
LED	Light-emitting Diode
JIS	Japanese Industrial Standard
M	Manual (Manual Exposure Mode)
SLR	Single Lens Reflex
TTL	Through the Lens
X	Xenon

Introduction

Calling the X-370 a beginner camera is, honestly, unfair because it could quite easily make a photographer of any skill level very happy. If you have arrived at this book because you have bought or received an X-370, here is the best takeaway I have for you: Nice. It's a good camera just as capable as almost every other Minolta SR-mount camera, and these have proven themselves to be reliable over the years. The X-370, though at the "bottom" of the X lineup, trounces the rest of the X cameras when it comes to interface simplicity, streamline, and functionality in a single camera. This is a great first, last, or first and last camera to use as you learn and master film photography.

This book's structure intends to help you learn your camera quickly and effectively. The goal: shorten your learning time and help you get to the important work of using your camera to learn photography, explore your creative vision, or enjoy the opportunity to shoot photos with it. Each chapter should give you the skills to be a better photographer. To help you find the information you need, this list provides each chapter's content:

"Chapter 1: The Minolta X-370 Details" lists some basic facts and figures about the camera and provides a background understanding of the camera itself.

"Chapter 2: What are the Buttons?" details the camera's interface elements and names the buttons and dials. This gives us a common language to talk about camera operations. Small interface elements, such as markings, that don't warrant their own sub-chapter are explained in Chapter 2.

"Chapter 3: Basic Operation" details the camera's basic operation and setup. These tasks help the camera take a photo. While it seems like a lot is here, once you have your camera set up most of these tasks are completed quickly.

"Chapter 4: Flash Basics" provides some basic tips and best practices on flash use. This receives its own chapter because many of my YouTube subscribers asked for flash use tips. This chapter should set you up to use a flash well and with some basic practices that help flatter your subject.

"Chapter 5: Reading the Light Meter" provides diagrams that clarify your light meter's information. Your light meter will tell you what you need to know to take a properly exposed photo.

"Chapter 6: Take a Photo" details the process of taking a photo. In general, this succeeds when everything this book covers to this point is set correctly.

"Chapter 7: Tips for the Minolta X-370" provides tips on using this camera effectively. Based on personal experience, these provide insights into ways of making your camera perform well.

"Chapter 8: Known Problems" lists known problems with this camera, their prognosis, remedies, and whether or not they can be worked around.

One last note, if you'd like to see the principles discussed in this book in use, I created a two-part video series about this model camera that overlaps this book's content significantly. The videos also have time-linked indices in the descriptions to help you find exactly the content you need. Here are links to those videos:

Minolta X-370 (X-300, Seagull DF-300) Tutorial Walkthrough Video Manual Review

https://youtu.be/aQK2830_Mss

Minolta X-370 (X-300) Batteries, Lenses, Load Film, Focusing, and Double Exposures

https://youtu.be/3Wic02SHkHY

1. The Minolta X-370 Details

1.1. Minolta X-370 Statistics at a Glance:

Shutter speeds: 1 second to 1/1,000th and Bulb

Flash sync speed: 1/60th with X flashes

Compatible flash types: X

Film speed range: 12-3200 with the in-camera light meter

Light meter type: Center-weighted with and LED-indicated shutter speed display

Lens mount: Minolta SR (commonly mis-named the MC or MD)

Focusing screen: Fixed split-prism with microprism collar

Battery type: Two 357-type

Dimensions: 141x91x57mm

Weight: 482 grams

Production years: 1984 to 1990 as the Minolta X-370 and X-300 and as the Seagull DF-300 (and many other variants we'll name in a moment) from 1997 to as recently as 2017.

Notable features: The Seagull DF-300 arose, apparently, when Minolta camera production outsourced to China and the Seagull camera company. Seagull was able to produce a re-badged (a term used when a product is released in near-identical form under another name) version called the Seagull DF-300, among others. All the Seagull-made re-badges are, to the best of my knowledge, identical in function and specifications to the X-370. Here are some re-badged versions of which I'm aware:

- Carena DF-300
- Centon DF-300
- Revue DF-300
- Samyang DF-400X
- Vivitar V50

In addition, the Minolta X-600 was primarily an X-370 with focus confirm capability and different batteries.

1.2. About the Minolta X-370

Konica Minolta released the X-370 (called the X-300 outside of North America) as an entry-tier 35mm interchangeable-lens single lens reflex (SLR) camera. That means the camera is geared toward beginner, student, and casual photographers, can take any 35mm film, and that lenses can be taken off and put back on when you aren't taking a photo without affecting the film or images.

The Minolta X-370 uses a center-weighted (C-W) through the lens (TTL) light meter. TTL means that the light passing through the lens is used by the light meter to determine exposure information. C-W meters, in general, measure all the light from the scene but bias the meter reading to the light level in the middle of the image. This can be a useful tip when taking a photo of someone as placing them in the center of the image will help ensure the photo of the person turns out well. The Minolta X-370's C-W meter is designed to attempt to make the scene a flat gray. That means that your dark areas will then be dark and light areas light; in general, C-W meters meters create proper tone and color rendition on film in most situations. Chapter 5, Reading the Light Meter, will provide details about how to read the light meter's display. Right now, you can see your light meter information in your camera's viewfinder.

While we're talking about the viewfinder, it reduces the image by 0.9X and has a 95% frame coverage. Those points mean that what you see in the viewfinder is 90% the size of what will reach the film plane and what is on your negative extends about 2.5% of the image's total width and height beyond the viewfinder's image. This allows you to fill the viewfinder frame completely and still have room to crop your image. If you want to see what that looks like, **Figure 1**

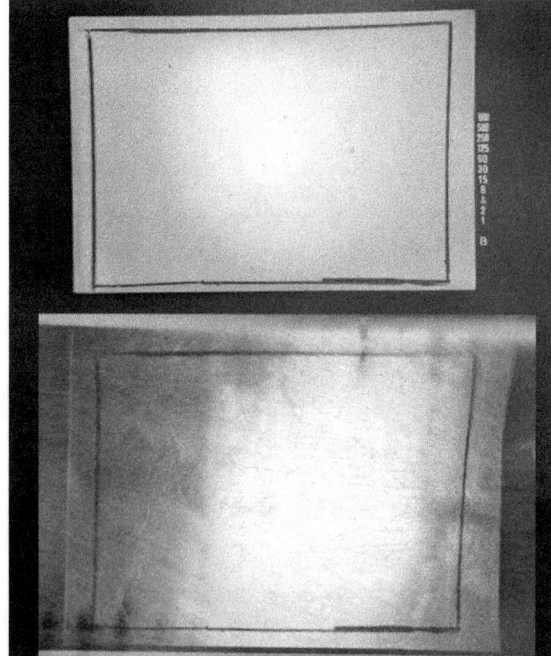

Figure 1: The viewfinder crops the image slightly to allow for corrections to the digital or print photo.

provides a photo of the viewfinder screen and the same scene projected through the camera's shutter curtain.

The focusing screen itself is fixed (it can't be removed without camera disassembly) and uses a matte field with a central split-prism and microprism collar to aid in fine focusing. The matte field is where you'll do most of the scene composition and you can use the microprism collar to verify focus and then recompose your image in the viewfinder. In the middle is a split prism focusing circle and it works by showing unfocused light as mis-aligned. That split prism indicates proper focus when the image in the top half aligns with the image in the lower half.

The Minolta X-370 has a $1/60^{th}$ of a second flash speed. This means that the camera can use a flash and have the image turn out suitably from $1/60^{th}$ of a second and slower. Faster shutter speeds will not work. Chapter 4, Flash Basics, covers flash use on your camera and provides some tips.

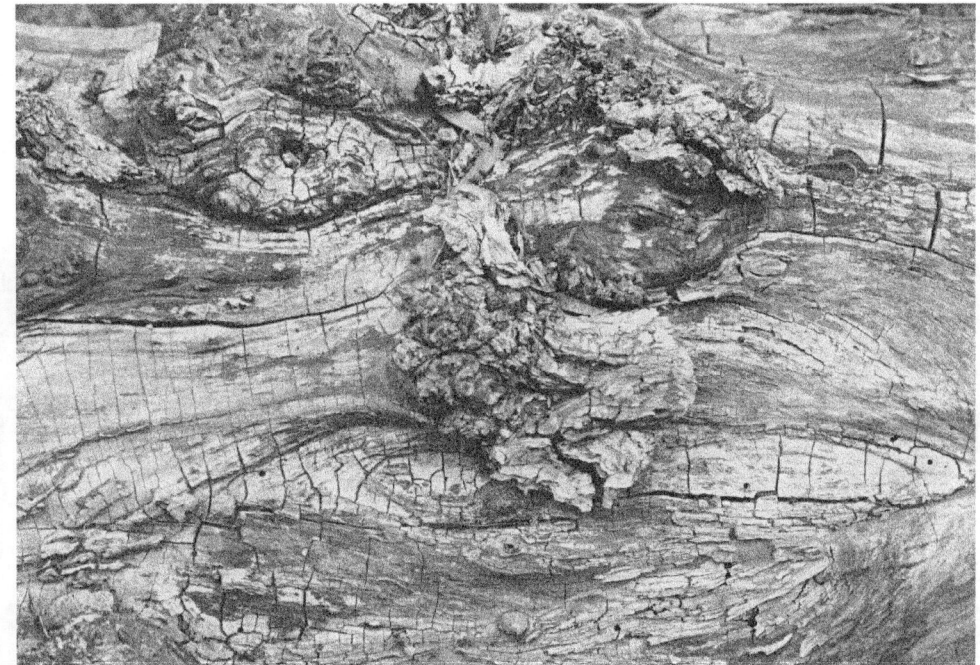

Minolta X-370 Variant | Minolta SR 50mm f/1.7 | Rollei Variochrome Film

2. What are the Buttons?

Welcome to Chapter Two! Understanding the Minolta X-370's background, let's dive into the camera's controls. This chapter labels and names the buttons. Subsequent chapters and sub-chapters detail what they do. This chapter also covers some basic items that don't warrant detailed discussion.

2.1. Top Controls

For the Minolta X-370, most image control occurs on the camera's top right. **Figure 2** details the names of the different top controls. I'll include larger versions of these images as we discuss the controls.

- A- Film Rewind and Back Release
- B- Power Switch
- C- Flash Hot Shoe
- D- Serial Number
- E- Flash Main Contact
- F- Flash Communication Contact
- G- Shutter Release and Shutter Speed Selector
- H- Shutter Speed Window
- I- Film Load Indicator
- J- Frame Count Window
- K- Film Advance Lever
- L- Film ISO Window
- M- Film ISO Dial Lock

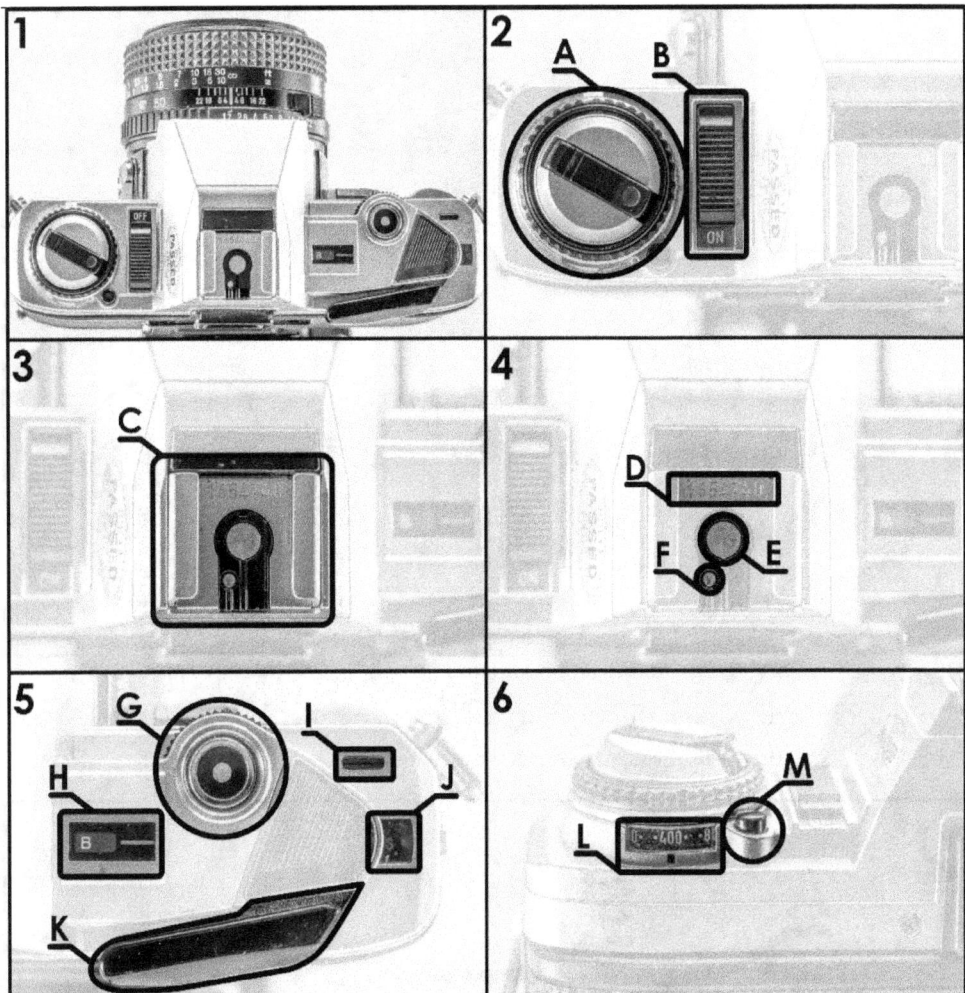

Figure 2: The top controls help determine image results.

The following paragraphs delve into each item labeled in Figure 2. The paragraphs will all begin with a larger version of Items 1 to 6 in Figure 2 and then detail the use and function for each labeled item.

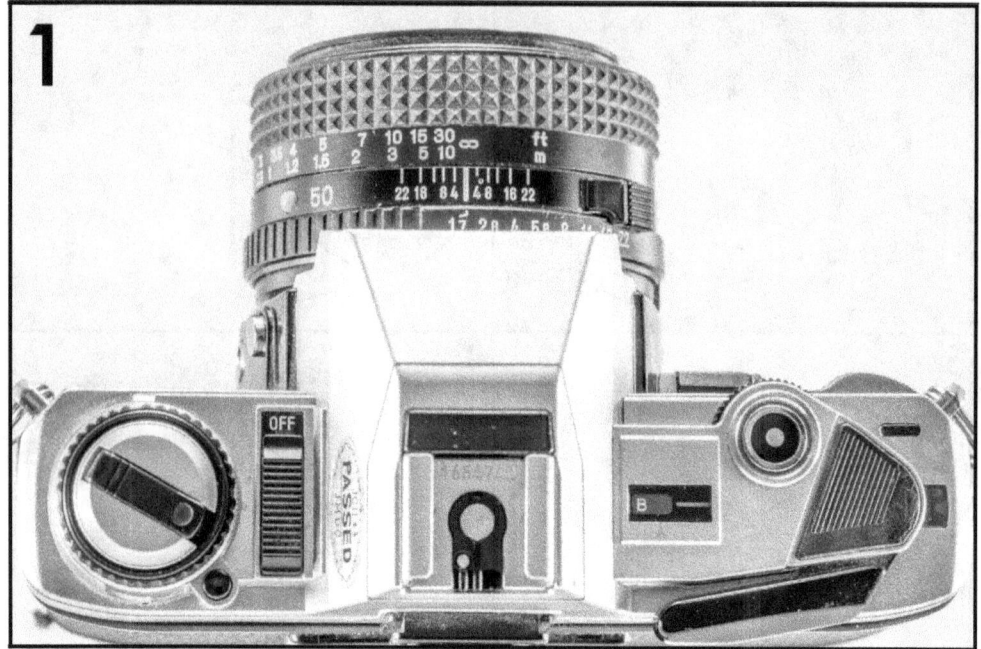

Figure 2-1 provides an overall view of the camera from the top. This is where very much of the work performed on this camera occurs. As you use these controls more, they will become more intuitive.

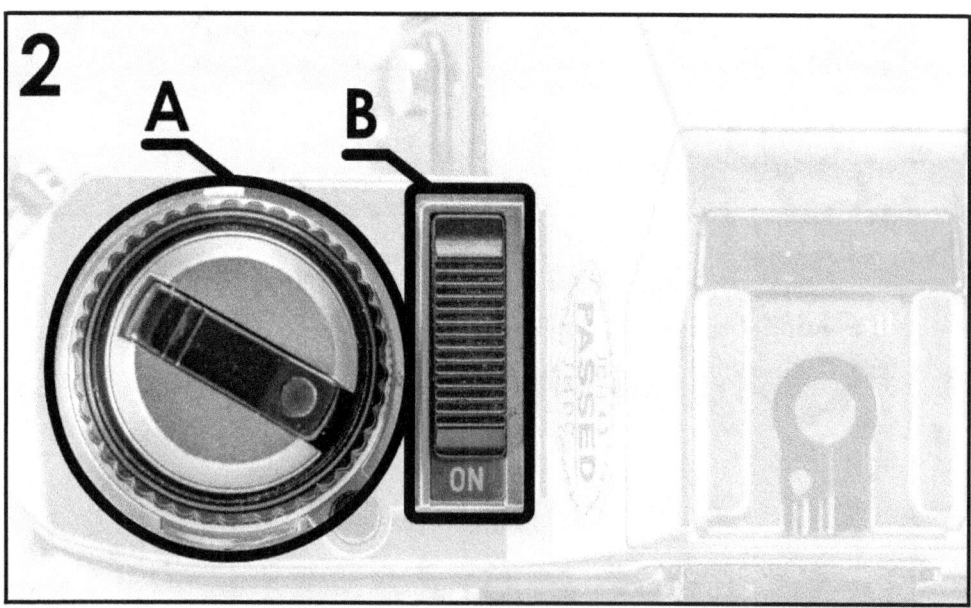

Figure 2-2 marks two items: A is the Film Rewind and Back Release. The film rewind knob and lever allow you to rewind your film when you finish a roll as well as take any slack out of the film for operations like multiple exposures (detailed later in this book.) When the lever is closed for photography, and when you advance the film, if you loaded the film correctly the knob will spin in the direction opposite the arrow. Chapter 3.2 shows this in use for rewinding film.

Item B, the Power Switch, turns the camera on and off. When off, the camera will preserve the battery and will not be able to accidentally take photos as the shutter button will not respond when pressed.

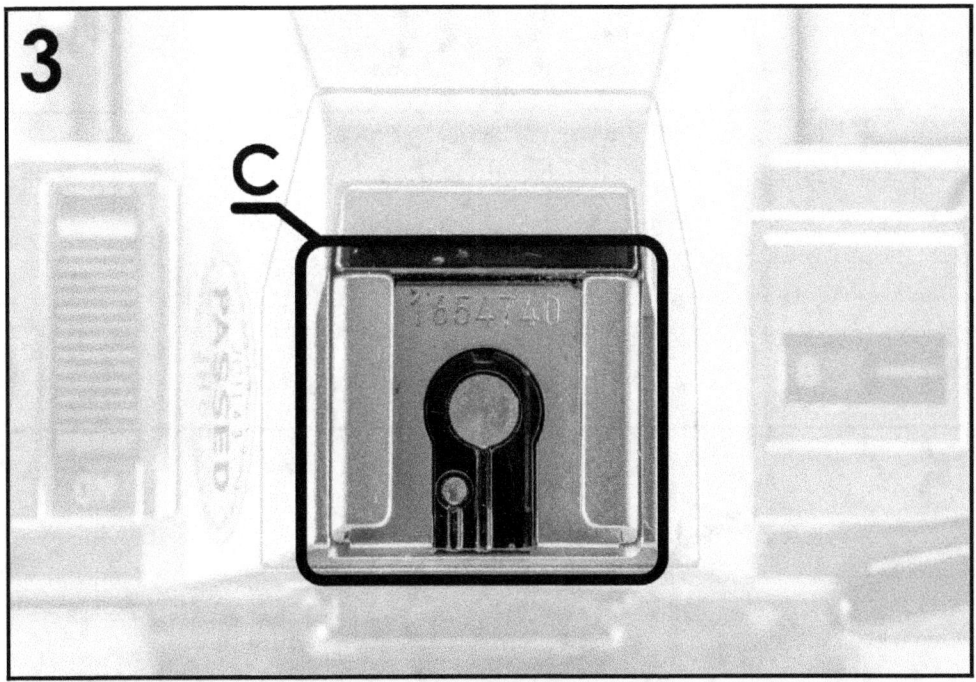

Figure 2-3 shows the camera's Hot Shoe, Item C. In a few pages we'll discuss adjusting the shutter speed, but for right now, the $1/60^{th}$ shutter speed on the X-370 is red. That coloration indicates that it is the fastest shutter speed at which a flash will work. This hot show is where the flash will be connected.

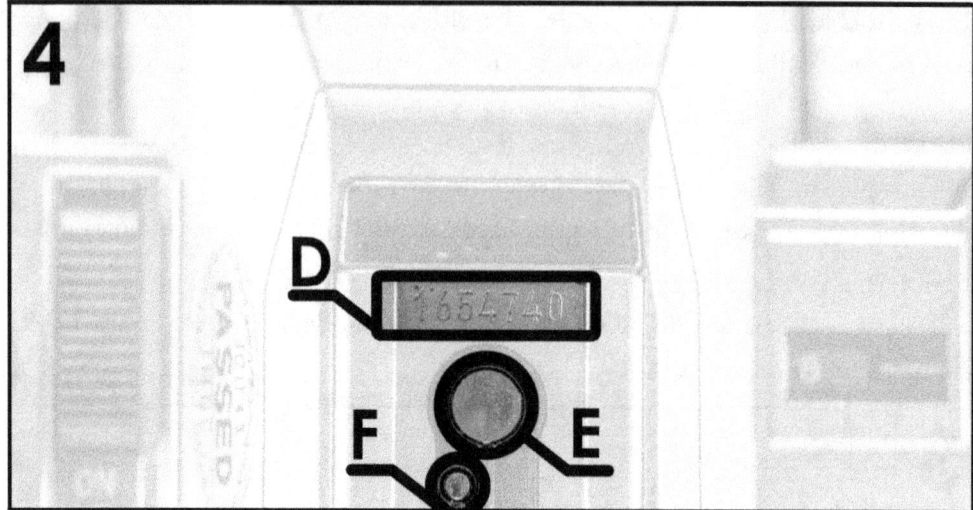

Figure 2-4 has three minor items. The serial number (Item D) identifies your camera as unique and yours. The silver discs (Item E, Flash Main Contact, and Item F, Flash Communication Contact) inside the hot shoe control the flash. Any flash with only a single contact on the foot will work with this camera. Fancier or more-expensive flashes with two or five contacts only know when to fire; those flashes will not have any automatic controls. If you buy a flash, choose an inexpensive one with manual power controls.

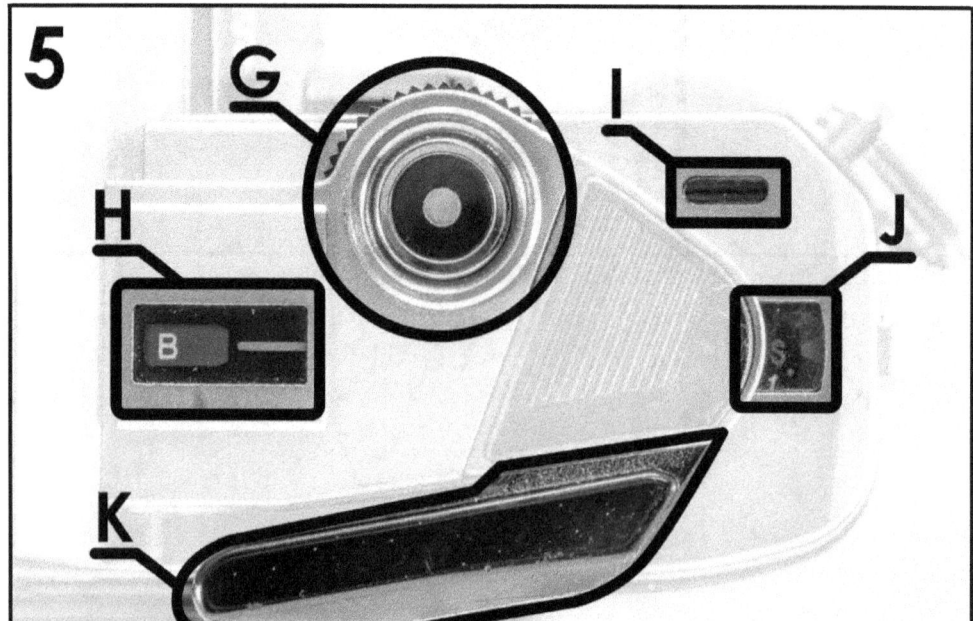

Figure 2-5 indicates many of the frequent controls used with the X-370. Item G has two items – the Shutter Release and Shutter Speed Selector. The camera's shutter button, the silver and black bullseye, triggers the camera's shutter to take a photo. In order for this to work, the film advance lever (Item K) has to have been advanced, the camera's power must be on, and the camera needs good batteries. Beneath the shutter release, a small wheel that looks a bit like a gear can be rotated in either direction to select shutter speeds.

The shutter speed dial controls your camera's shutter speed – the time that the film is exposed to light. Item H is the Shutter Speed Window and displays the selected shutter speed. See the red line on the window's right side? That's the shutter speed index and indicates the selected shutter speed. All of the shutter speeds except three are fractional seconds, those being the "1", "B", and "AUTO". Where the camera reads "1000", that shutter speed is $1/1,000^{th}$ of a second. Where the camera reads "15", that is a $1/15^{th}$ of a second shutter speed, so a much longer shutter time. Guess what the "2" and the "60" indicate. If you guessed 1/2 second and $1/60^{th}$ of a second, respectively, that's correct.

The "1" is a full-second exposure and the "B" stands for bulb. Bulb is an antiquated photography term for the shutter speed used for flash photography more than a century ago. In bulb, the camera will keep the shutter open as long as you hold the shutter button down. A locking cable release can work well for long photographs, like overnight star trails photos.

You may have noticed that the 60 is red. That speed is your flash sync speed. Chapter 4 covers this in detail. The key point is: $1/60^{th}$ is the fastest shutter speed at which a flash will work properly on the X-370. If you use a faster shutter speed, for instance $1/500^{th}$, your photo will not be fully illuminated by the flash. Longer shutter speeds, such as $1/15^{th}$ and "B" also work for flash use.

Lastly, let's discuss AUTO mode. AUTO mode is, in technical terms, aperture-priority mode. In this mode, you select AUTO on the shutter speed dial, set your aperture (on the camera lens, which we'll discuss later) and then the camera will pick the best shutter speed for your photo. If the aperture, film, and light available for the photo mean that a shutter speed faster than $1/1,000^{th}$ of a second is required, because the camera cannot achieve that shutter speed it provides a warning LED in the viewfinder. That LED, a small, red triangle above the number scale, flashes if a smaller aperture opening (larger aperture number) is required for the photo.

Item I is a simple informational item that confirms if film is or is not present in the camera. When the window is all black, as shown in Figure 2-5, then no film is loaded in the camera. When film has been loaded, an orange flag appears in that window and that flag moves from left to right as the film is used. This provides quick confirmation of film presence as well as approximately how much of the film roll has been used.

Item J builds on this and indicates the specific frame the camera is on. The camera, for reasons we'll detail in Chapter 3.2, starts your frame counting at -2, marked by a red "S" for start. The orange triangle on the right side of the numbers indicates which frame you are on. Film today comes in 24- and 36- exposure rolls. The frame counter lets you know how many photos you've taken and how many are left so you can plan your film use.

Lastly in Figure 2-5, Item K is the Film Advance Lever. The film advance lever advances the film (more on this in Chapter 3.2) after each shot. At the same time that the film is advanced, the lever also re-arms the shutter for the next photo. This action tensions the springs and mechanisms in the camera so that it can take another photo.

Ideally, the film advance lever should be moved in a single, smooth, and uninterrupted stroke from start to finish. If you do accidentally let go of the lever mid-stroke, simply finish the action until the lever meets resistance. It happens and the camera will be fine.

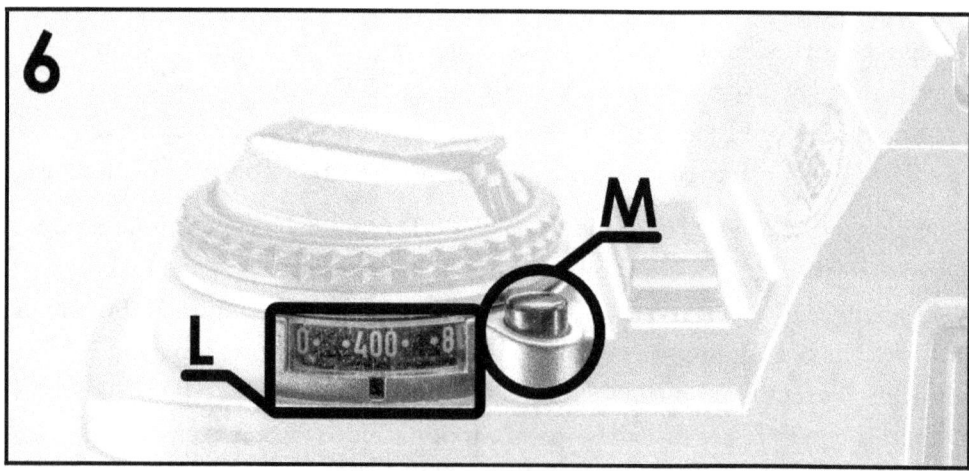

In **Figure 2-6**, Item L is the Film ISO Window and Item M the Film ISO Dial Lock. Depressing the lock button allows the knurled ring around the film rewind to spin, which adjusts the camera's sensitivity to light. The numbers on the dial that spins with that ring correspond to film speed numbers.

To obtain a proper exposure, the camera needs an important data point from you when you load film: the ISO. This dial allows you to tell the camera what speed film you're using. You will input the film's ISO each time you load film, unless it's already set to the right speed. When this camera was made, the American Standards Association (ASA) governed film speeds. When ASA stopped setting the standard, ISO took over and adopted the ASA and German *Deutsches Institut für Normung* (DIN) film speeds as their standards. ISO and ASA are the same. If you have a 400 ISO film set your camera's ASA to 400.

2.2. Front Controls

The Minolta X-370 has only a few controls on the camera's front. This chapter will discuss what each control is used for or where to find additional information on the specific control. **Figure 3** provides a markup of the camera's front controls.

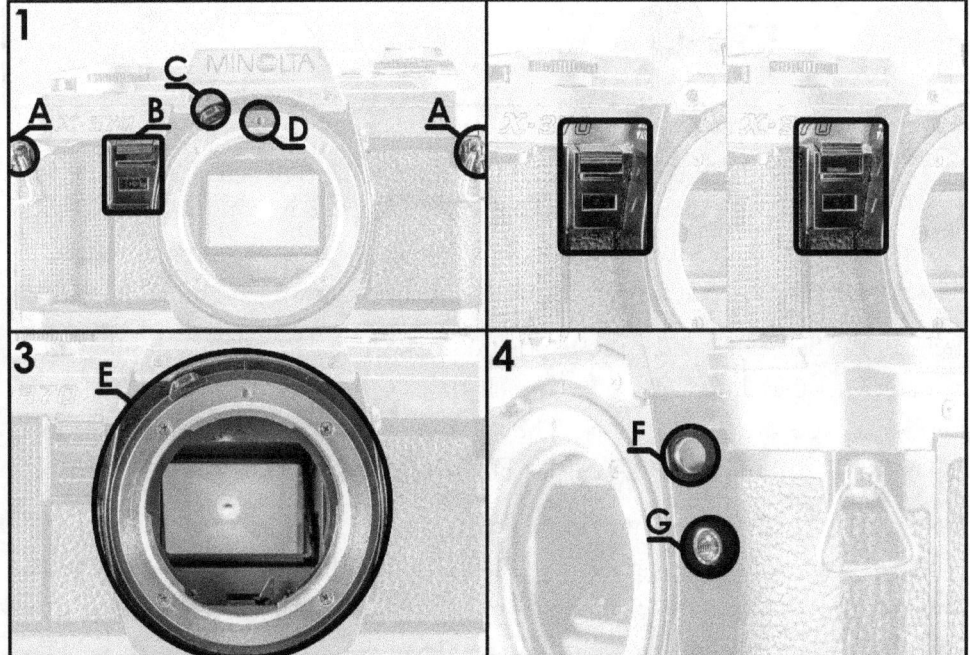

Figure 3: The front controls affect photos less often.

A- Strap Lugs

B- Self-timer and Auto-exposure Lock Switch

C- Lens Meter Interface Coupling Lever

D- Lens Mounting Index

E- Lens Mount Flange

F- Lens Release Button

G- Cable Release Socket

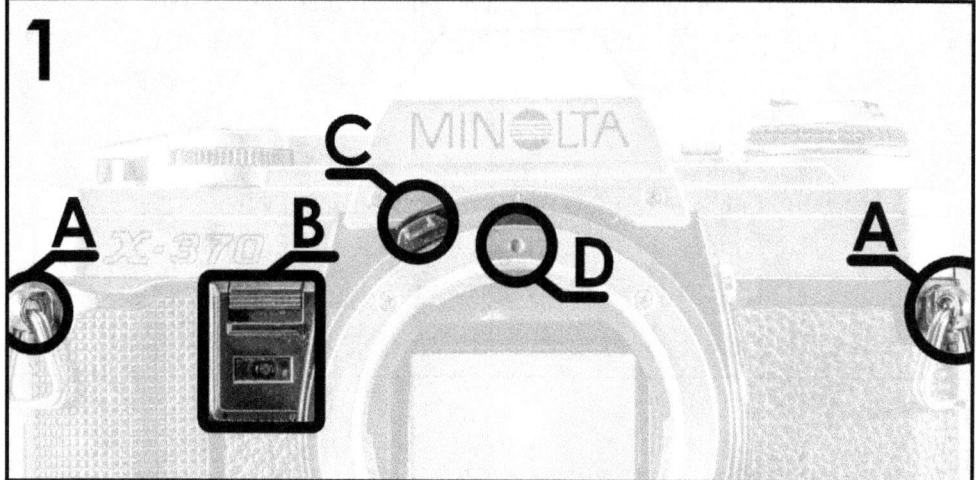

Figure 3-1 details the primary controls on the camera's front. Your camera has two lugs for your strap (Item A). If you're missing the split rings, any round split ring will do. Split rings can damage your camera's finish and it's worth either putting some thick tape on the camera's body or getting some shrink-wrap tube to put over your strap and split rings if you want to protect the finish.

Item B, the Self-timer and Auto-exposure Lock (AEL) Switch, is a combination switch that, when lifted, activates the self-timer and, when pressed and held, performs exposure memory lock. The latter item deserves some discussion so the text following Figure 3-2 explains how this switch works.

Item C is the Lens Meter Interface Coupling Lever and it has a single job – connect to a lever on the camera lens. The lever on the lens rotates as the lens' aperture ring is adjusted – check this on your lens and you can see how the aperture ring moves the lever and how that lever connects to your camera. The Minolta X-370 allows something called open-aperture metering. This means that the camera knows these facts about your lens when it's mounted:

1- The lens' fastest aperture setting (the iris is fully open; the lowest number on the lens' aperture ring.)
2- What the lens aperture is set to (without the aperture having to actually close.)

The camera knows this by the placement of this ring and a connection pin inside of the lens mount (not shown in these photos and, unless you plan to repair cameras, also not vital information.) These data points let the camera determine a proper exposure (shutter speed and aperture) along with the film speed and available light, and it does all of this through levers and switches. Honestly, kinda cool and it says a lot about the creativity of early SLR engineers who figured these things out in the 1950s – decades before this camera was made.

Lastly in Figure 3-1, Item D is the Lens Mounting Index. This index is used to align lenses for mounting (more on this in Chapter 3.3.)

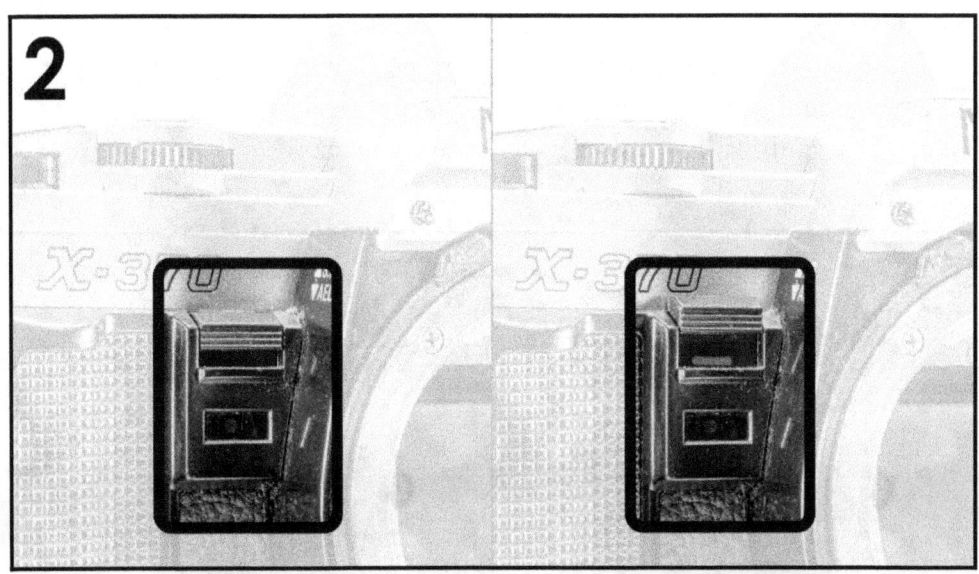

Let's discuss the self-timer and AEL shown in **Figure 3-2**. An indicator on the side of your camera's mount provides a reminder of this switch's functions. An up triangle indicates "S.T." for self-timer and a down-triangle indicates "AEL", which we defined earlier.

As we touched on briefly, lifting the lever activates a ten-second self-timer countdown with a light that blinks to provide an indication of the self-timer being active and how far along the count has progressed. At the end of the count-down, the camera will take a photo.

The AEL button has a different function. One key note about the AEL button, it only works when the camera is in AUTO mode. If you manually select a shutter speed yourself, this button has no functionality. Using your film's speed and available light, the camera will calculate an exposure and select a shutter speed that will provide a proper exposure – an appropriate amount of light reaches the film. Film is discussed in more detail in Chapter 3.2, but in short for right now, film is designed to receive a set amount of light to deliver a proper exposure. A 100 ISO film needs more light than a 400 ISO film, for instance. Your light meter knows this and it also knows how much light is coming in through the lens. If you point the camera at a dark corner of a room, it might indicate you need to use f/1.7 and ¼ of a second for your exposure settings. If you point it outside your window on a sunny day, it might indicate f/16 and 1/250th of a second. With the AEL button, you can press it while you have one of those two scenes in the frame, hold the button down, and take your photo with a different composition and as long as you have held the button in place to remember the original settings. Chapter 7.1 covers and example where this would be useful. For now, the key takeaways on this button are that it remembers automatic exposure settings when light levels change and it needs to be held in place because releasing it will erase the memory.

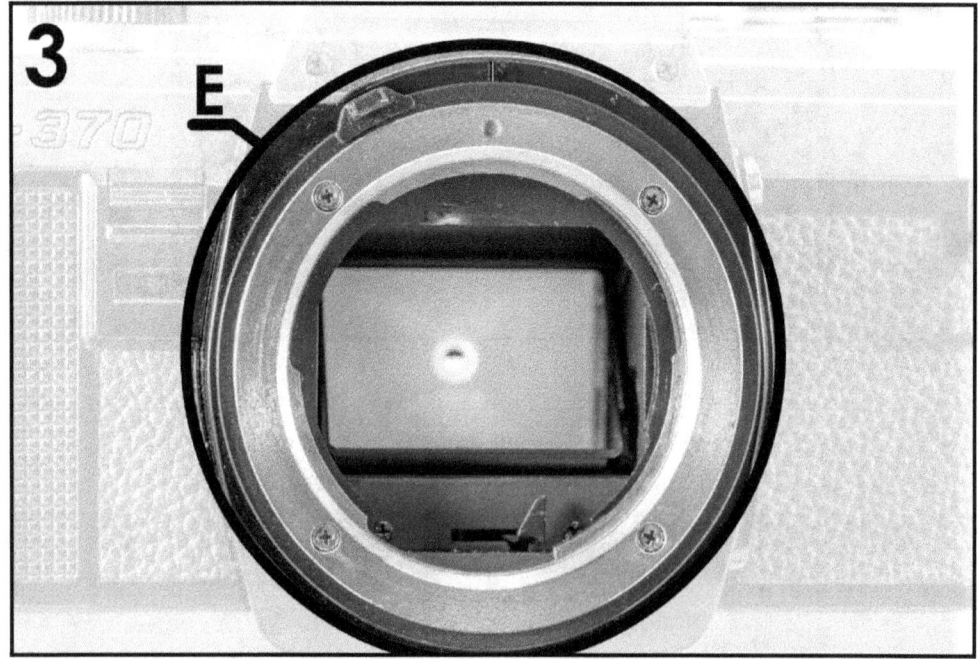

Item E in **Figure 3-3** is the Lens Mount Flange. Chapter 3.3 discusses lens changes in detail. For now, the important note about this part is that this camera uses Minolta SR-mount lenses. Later versions of the SR-mount lenses are often called MC and MD, often erroneously called MC or MD *mount*. All MC and MD lenses are SR-mount. Your Minolta X-370 can use any SR-mount lens from the oldest to the newest. If you want to find another lens for your camera, you can look for Minolta SR, MC, and MD mount lenses as common search terms. Minolta AF, A, Maxxum, Dynax, and Alpha lenses will not fit this camera.

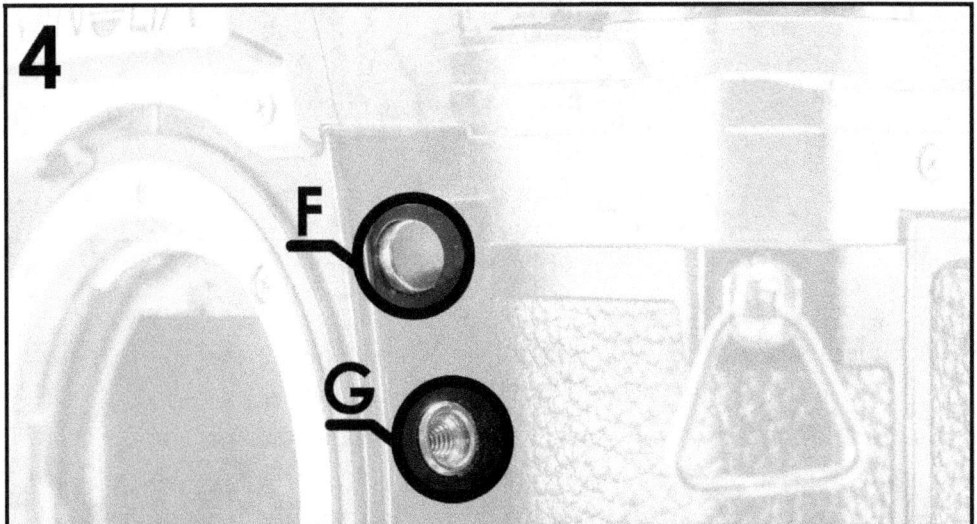

Figure 3-4 shows two items, the Lens Release Button (Item F) and the Cable Release Socket (Item G). The lens release button needs to be pressed to remove a lens from the camera (Chapter 3.3). The cable release socket allows you to use a threaded cable release instead of pressing the shutter button. A cable release will let you take photos without the risk of the action of pressing the shutter button shaking the camera. This is a technique meant to be used in concert with a tripod for long-exposures, macro photography that is highly susceptible to camera shake affecting image quality, even portraits if you're in a studio and want to stand next to your camera instead of behind it to make your model feel more comfortable. Cable releases are an optional accessory and the threaded variety all used a standard thread so any will work.

2.3. Back Controls

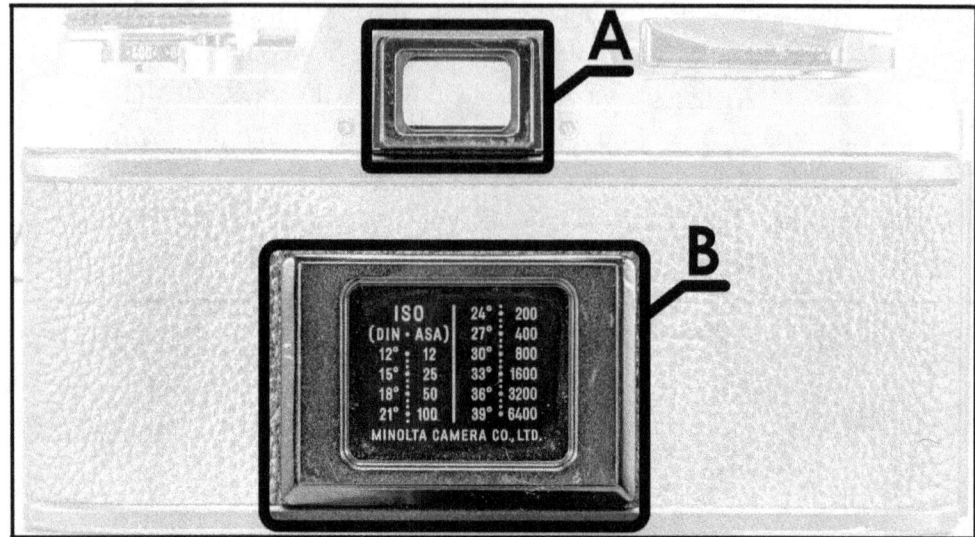

Figure 4: The back controls help with image composition.

The Minolta X-370 has very few controls on the camera's back, just the Viewfinder Eyepiece (Item A) and the Film Memo Holder (Item B). If you take a look at your viewfinder eyepiece from above you might notice some grooves on the sides. Those are for mounting accessories like diopter adjusters, eyecups, and right-angle viewfinders. For the film memo holder, when you open the box that your 35mm film comes in, tear off the top box flap and slide it in here through the top. That will remind you what type of film you have and the number of frames on the roll. **Figure 4** indicates the rear controls.

2.4. Bottom Controls

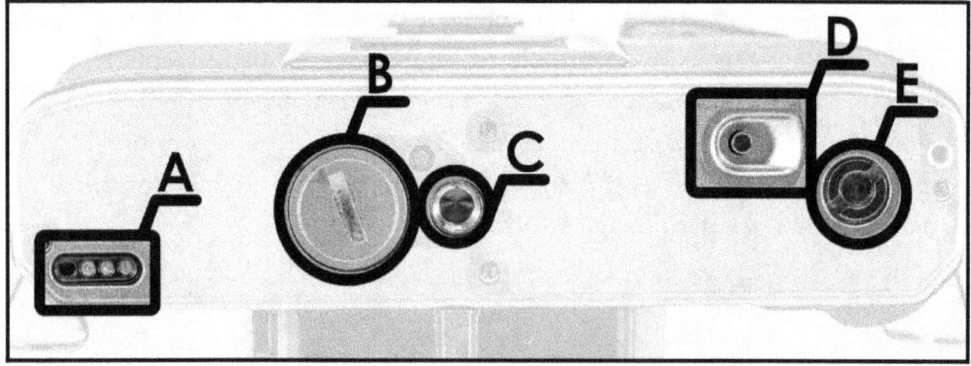

Figure 5: The elements on the camera's bottom help with specific tasks.

The Minolta X-370 has a few items of note on the bottom, shown in **Figure 5**. These are not controls that you use often, or specifically to affect camera operation when taking a photo, but they do give you the ability to take better photos and use the camera.

- A- Motor Drive Electronic Contacts
- B- Battery Cap
- C- Tripod Socket
- D- Film Rewind Release Button
- E- Motor Drive Mechanical Coupling

Item A, the Motor Drive Electronic Contacts, and Item E, the Motor Drive Mechanical Coupling, work together if your camera is outfitted with a motor drive. Motor drives do advance the film for you, but they also add a lot of bulk and weight. In general, if you don't have a motor drive, there's no reason to seek one out.

Item B, the Battery Cap, protects and encloses the battery chamber. Chapter 3.1 discusses batteries in detail.

The Tripod Socket, Item C, is a standard 1/4-20 socket and it allows you to connect the camera to a tripod or quick-release plate. This allows you to take stable photos at shutter speeds longer than the speeds you can hand-hold the camera at.

The Film Rewind Release Button, Item D, will need to be pressed for film rewinding. Not engaging the film rewind button and rewinding your film can cause damage to your camera's mechanisms or the film, or both.

2.5. *Film Chamber (Inside)*

Having seen the camera's external controls, let's look inside. To open your camera, lift the film rewind knob and the back should pop open easily. **Figure 6** demonstrates how to open the camera and the inside workings.

- A- Film Cassette Chamber
- B- Shutter Area
- C- Film Guide Rail
- D- Film Tension Sprocket
- E- Film Take-up Spool
- F- Film Pressure Plate
- G- Cassette Position Spring

Unmarked in Figure 6, the camera has light seals in the channels on the body, where the film door nests when closed. The compressible light seals, foam when the camera was made, help the camera's film door seal and ensure that no light leaks into the camera to fog or streak your film.

Cameras with yarn light seals had the original seals replaced; yarn light seals will likely outlast the camera. Foam light seals that become gooey, damaged, or dry and powdery should be replaced. The David Hancock Channel's video "Fast, Quick, and Permanent Camera Light Seal Replacement using Cotton Yarn" (https://youtu.be/Tfk0Si1Bvq8) shows this easy, five-minute fix.

Everything inside the camera is designed to give you the best images you can achieve. On the left, the Film Cassette Chamber (Item A) is where we'll load the film for the camera in Chapter 3.2.

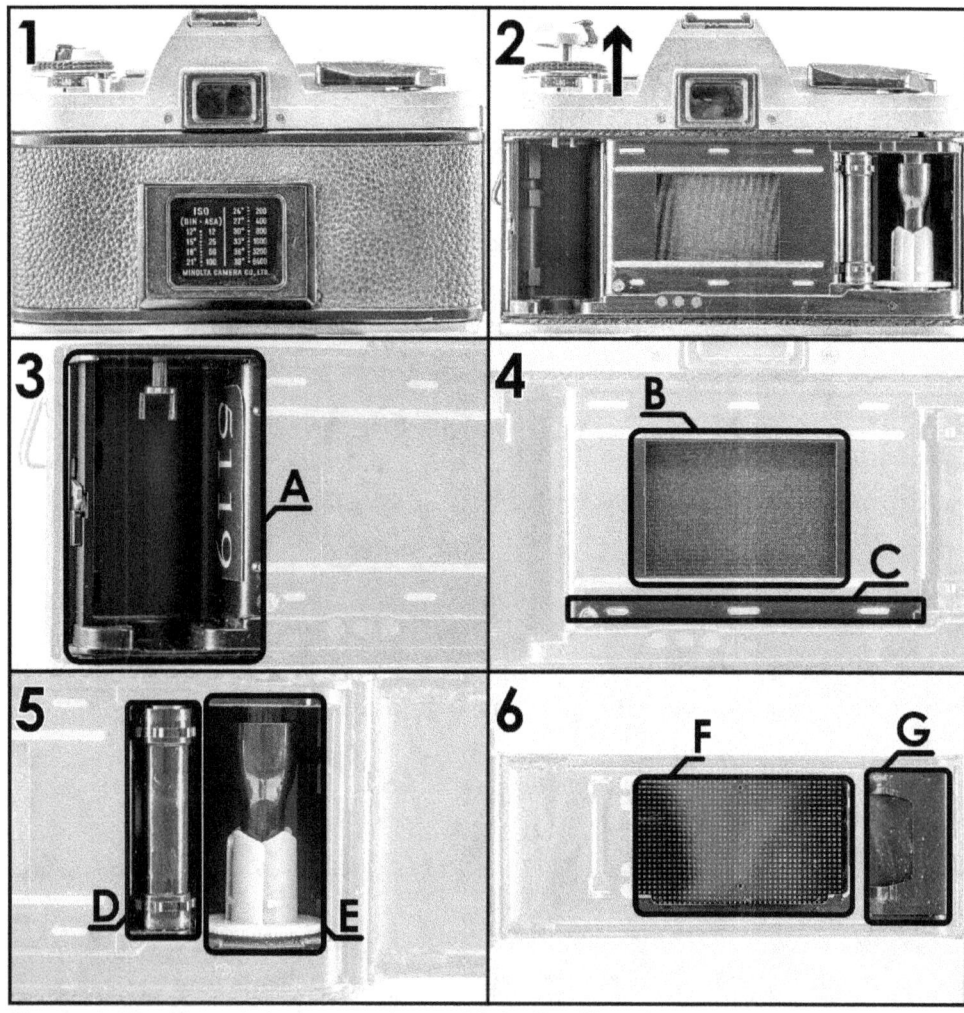

Figure 6: Significant design work went into the film chamber.

In the middle of your camera, the Shutter Area (Item B) has a light-proof shutter that opens and closes at the selected shutter speed to control the light reaching your film and deliver a proper exposure. That curtain allows lens changes to be done without ruining the film.

The four silver Film Guide Rails (Item C) in the camera ensure focused and aligned photos. The film rests between the outside two rails. The film's sprocket holes rest on the inside rails. With the film door closed, the Film Pressure Plate (Item F), in conjunction with those guide rails, keeps your film flat so that the lens focuses light properly.

The film take-up area consists of two rollers. On the left, the Film Tension Sprocket (Item D) pulls the film smoothly and prevents jamming (Chapter 3.2.) On the right, the Film Take-up Spool (Item E) collects and winds the exposed film.

The film door has a few components that help your camera work properly. The Film Pressure Plate (Item F) sandwiches the film flat to the image-recording plane, allowing lenses to focus light properly. Also on the right side of the door, a small, flat Film Cassette Positioning Spring (Item G) keeps the film cassette properly aligned so that film moves through the camera smoothly.

3. Basic Operation

3.1. Change the Battery

The Minolta X-370 uses two 357-type batteries (AG13, LR44, A76, S76, and 303 are other names.) Batteries can last a year and power all camera functions.

A quick note on batteries: off-brand 357 batteries are prone to swelling or bursting, both of which can damage your camera. Buy batteries from a major label (I use Duracell almost exclusively; Energizer, Sanyo, and Panasonic batteries are also good.) Avoid the no-name batteries that cost a fraction of good batteries; swollen or burst battery repair will cost as much as two or three decades' worth of good batteries. **Figure 7** shows how to change the battery:

1- Locate the battery chamber.
2- A good battery cap may have minor wear but no coin slot damage.
3- Remove the battery cap. The cap should unscrew easily.
4- A clean battery cap and chamber show no crystallized white or green powder. If needed, The David Hancock Channel has a video on cleaning battery chamber corrosion. (https://youtu.be/IeNM9usMY1Q)
5- The batteries, properly placed, should seat firmly and securely.
6- The battery cap includes markings that indicate the battery orientation.

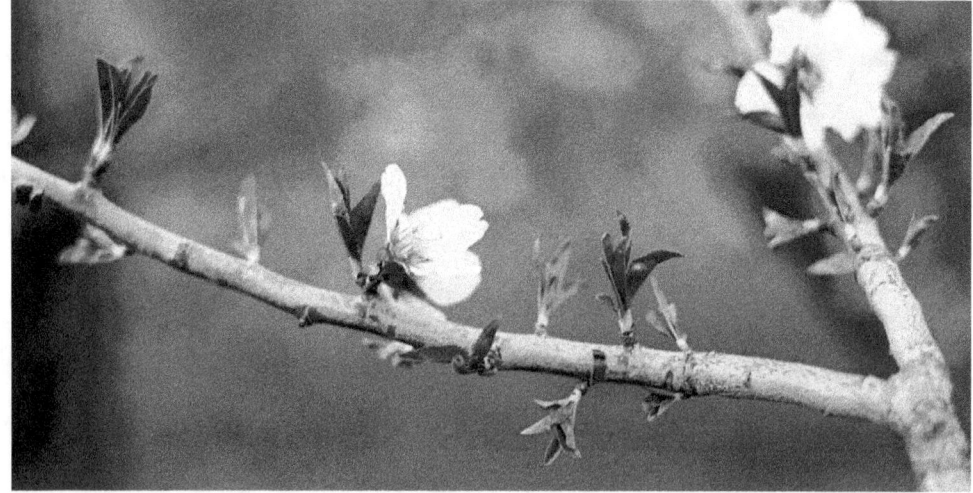

Minolta X-370 Variant | Minolta SR 50mm f/1.7 | Kodak Ektar Film

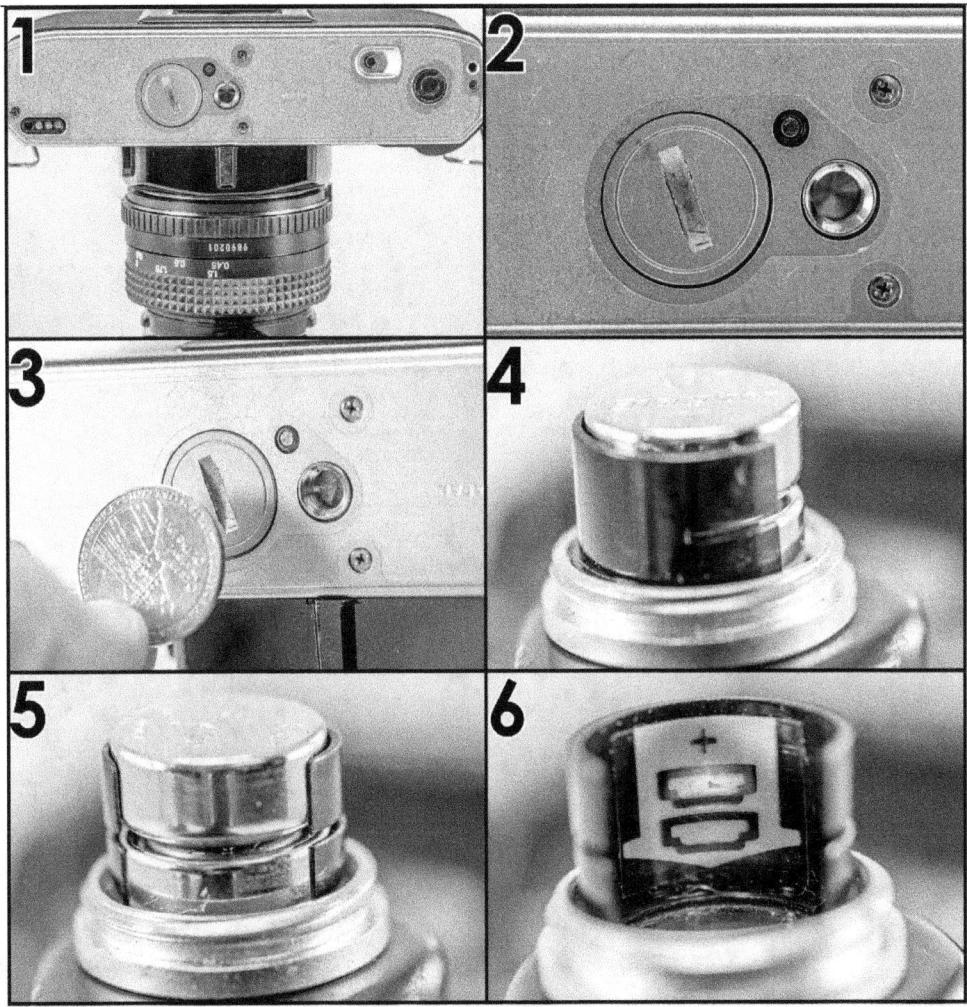

Figure 7: Make sure to use two 357-type batteries.

3.2. Film Loading

The Minolta X-370 takes 35mm film from 12-3200 ISO in third stops. What does that mean? Film speeds such as 100, 200, and 400 are each separated by a stop. The photographic term "stop" is where you stop an adjustment to control the light reaching your film. Confusingly, it applies to many things (film speeds, shutter speeds, aperture settings, and flash power.) The term's specifics are beyond this book's scope; what you need to know now is that doubling or halving the film speed, 100 to 200 or 400 to 200, is a single stop.

A third of a stop is between the full-stop markings. For instance, 100 to 125 ISO is a third-stop. 125 to 160 ISO is another third-stop. If you load your camera with Kodak Portra 160, set the ASA dial to the second dot going from 100 to 200 ASA. Remember, ASA and ISO are the same value. The film-loading process is easy. **Figures 8 and 9** break it into granular steps. Once done a few times, it should take around 15 seconds to swap out film.

If you have never used film before, film is one and done: it can record light to create an image once. If you open the camera's back with film outside the cassette (on the take-up spool), you will erase many if not all your photos. Once you close the film back, leave it closed until you finish your film and rewind it.

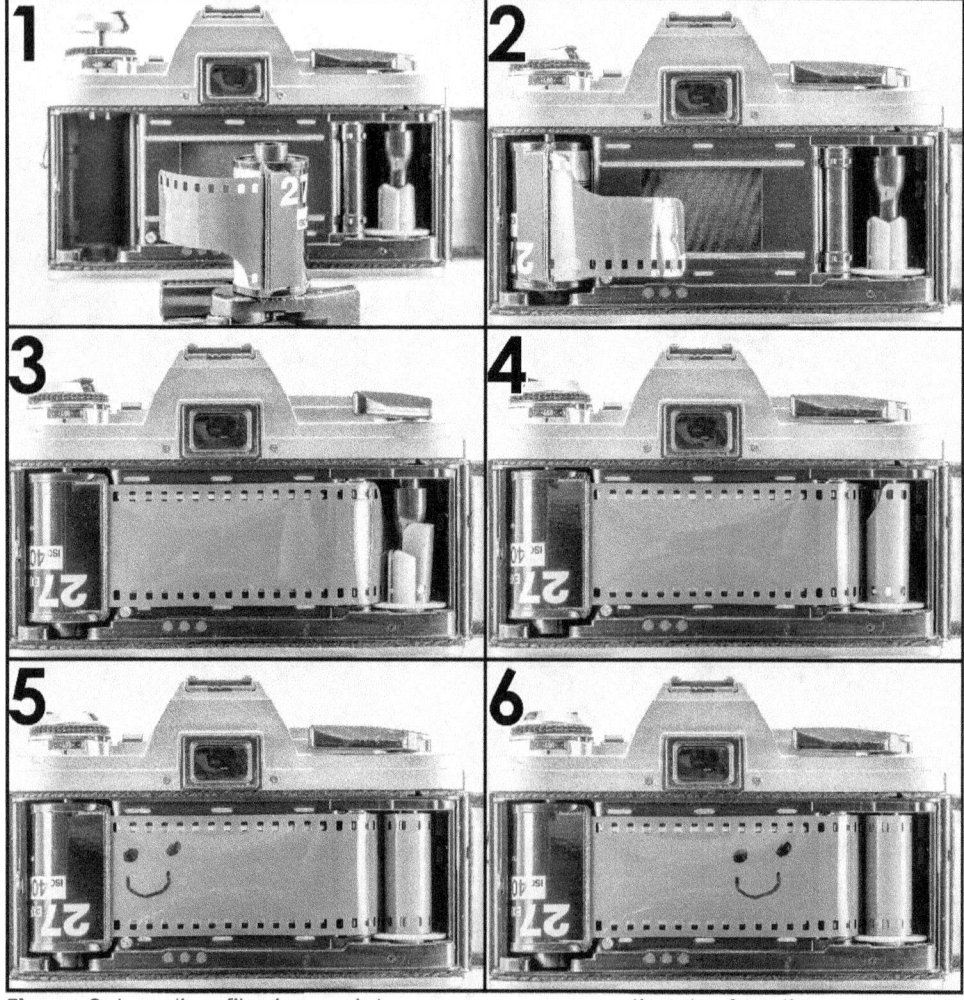

Figure 8: Loading film is a quick process once practiced a few times.

1- Lift the rewind knob until the door opens to load the film.
2- Any 35mm film will work in the Minolta X-370.
3- Load the film with the rewind knob raised then push the knob flush with the camera's body.
4- Push the film leader into the take-up spool.
5- Press the shutter button and advance the film advance lever once. The film should be taken up smoothly and easily by the take-up spool.
6- The smiley face demonstrates the film moving in the camera.
7- When you close the film door, the frame counter will rest on "S". Advance the film (fire the shutter button and then use the film advance lever) two or three times.
8- Start shooting at frame 1. Not all cameras give a complete frame 0 and losing half a frame on a good shot isn't preferable. So, as a best practice, start at frame 1.
9- Your shutter speed dial here is set to AUTO and with the X-370 this can slow the film loading process because the camera will fire a shutter speed appropriate for the light levels even before frame 1.
10- To avoid accidentally having very long shutter speeds when advancing to frame 1, set the dial to $1/1,000^{th}$ and, if you're using AUTO, return it to AUTO after reaching frame 1.
11- Change the ASA dial to your film's ISO. Start by pressing and holding the film speed dial lock release button.
12- Turn the film speed dial in the appropriate direction until you reach your desired film speed.

ASA and ISO are the same rating. Your ASA needs to remain the same for the entire roll. Changing that setting during shooting will result in some images turning out poorly. Film can be developed once and as a whole roll. If you change the ASA during your roll, some photos will not receive the proper light for the developing process. This could ruin your images.

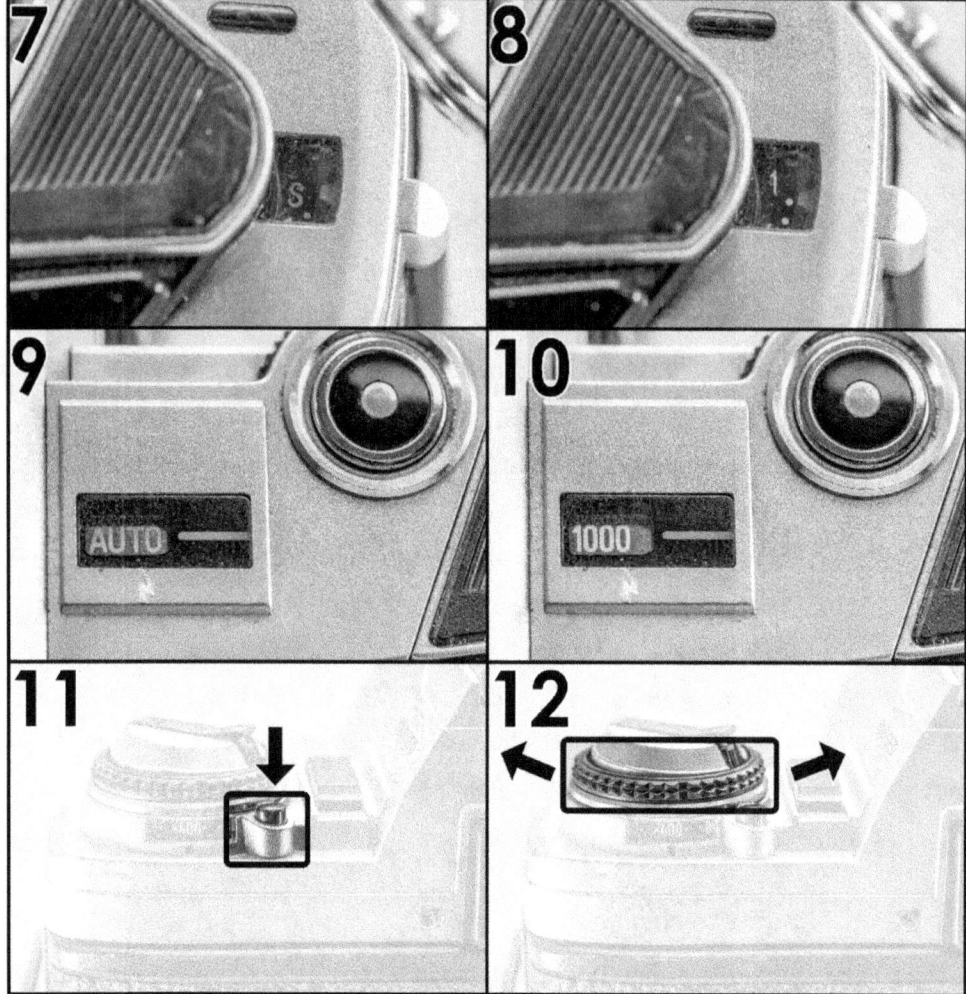

Figure 9: Loading film is a quick process once practiced a few times.

Following the loading process, turn your film rewind knob in the arrow's direction until slight resistance. Don't over-crank it. Winding to resistance confirms proper loading and helps keep the film flat for proper image focus.

Remember, don't open your camera to check on the film. It will do its thing. Keep the film door closed until you've taken all your photos and have completely rewound the film. Rewinding the film is done easily by pressing the film rewind button (we saw this on the bottom of the camera earlier in the book) and turning the film rewind lever in the arrow's direction. Film rewind tension and sound change when the film is fully rewound.

3.3. Lens Mounting and Unmounting

The Minolta X-370 allows you to change lenses when you're not taking a photo with no risk to your film. This allows you to carry different lenses and create different image looks on the same film. Swapping lenses is very easy because this camera has a bayonet mount. **Figure 10** shows how to swap a lens.

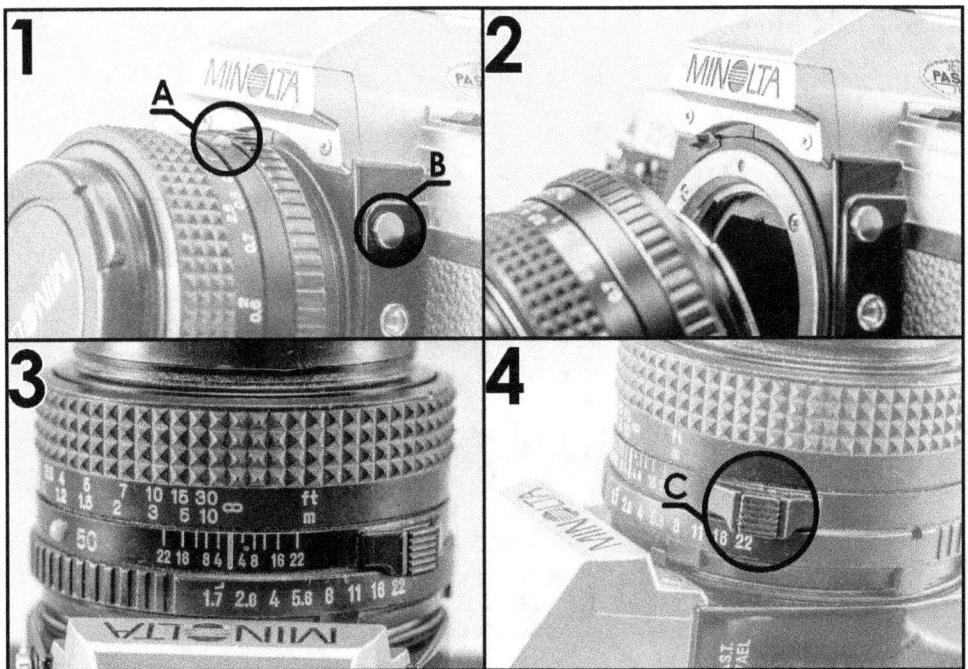

Figure 10: Changing a lens can be done without looking at it.

Here's a 50mm lens mounted on the camera.

1- To unlock the lens, press the lens release button (B) and rotate the lens until the lens mount index on the lens aligns as shown (A).

2- Pull the lens away from the camera to remove it.

3- To mount a new lens, align the red dot on the lens flange with the red dot on the camera's mount and reverse the removal process. A properly-mounted lens looks like this with the white focus point and aperture indicator centered on top. The lens will click into place.

4- Some lenses have a switch here (C) that, when pushed toward the camera, reveals a green mark. This switch only works with the Minolta X-700 and using it on your X-370 will cause your images to be severely underexposed (dark.)

Lenses are valuable and dropping one can be expensive. Be sure to keep a good grip on your lens when you remove it and secure it before grabbing the other lens you want to mount.

3.4. Focusing a Lens

Figure 11 shows a typical lens for this camera and indicates the key components. The Minolta X-370 is easy to focus: simply look through the viewfinder and rotate the Focus Ring (A) until the thing that you want to have be in focus is. The Focusing Scales (B) and Aperture Ring (C) indicate how much of the scene is in focus.

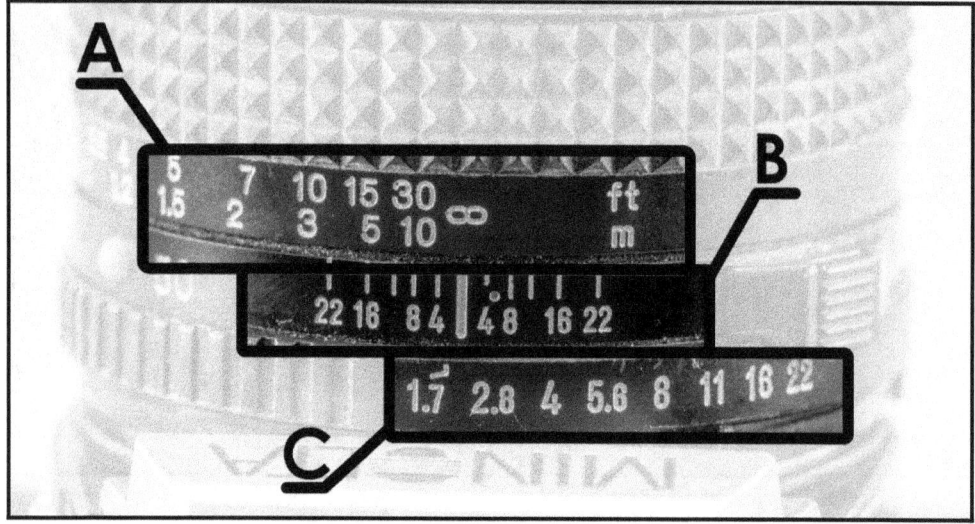

Figure 11: A standard lens provides needed information.

Turning the focusing ring changes the focal point from infinity focus to the closest focus point (different for each lens) and anywhere in between. A technical, usability definition for infinity focus is the lens' focal length times anywhere from 200 to 400, depending on lens maker. Using a factor of 400, this 50mm lens has an infinity focus point of 20,000 millimeters – 20 meters. The distance markers on this lens support that math.

Adjusting the aperture ring closes an iris in the lens during exposure. Removing the lens from your camera and setting it to f/16 or f/22, the iris should close to a small hole. Looking at the closed iris, adjust the aperture ring through all the stops and notice that as the numbers on the ring decrease the opening increases. The smaller the iris opening, the more of the scene in front of the camera that will be in focus.

To demonstrate this, between the aperture ring and the focus ring you'll see a set of numbers and lines, the focusing scales, and distance markers. The distance markers change when the lens is focused; the focusing scales are fixed. Set your lens aperture f/16 and place the infinity focus point (∞) above the 16. That row of numbers, mirrored on the lens in Figure 11 from 22 to 22, represents what is in focus when aligning the distance and aperture settings. So if your infinity focus is set above 16 and your aperture is set to f/16, then everything from infinity to the focus point above the other 16 marker will be in focus. Knowing now how to read the information on the lens, you can compose images with proper focus and focal depth and know why those images work.

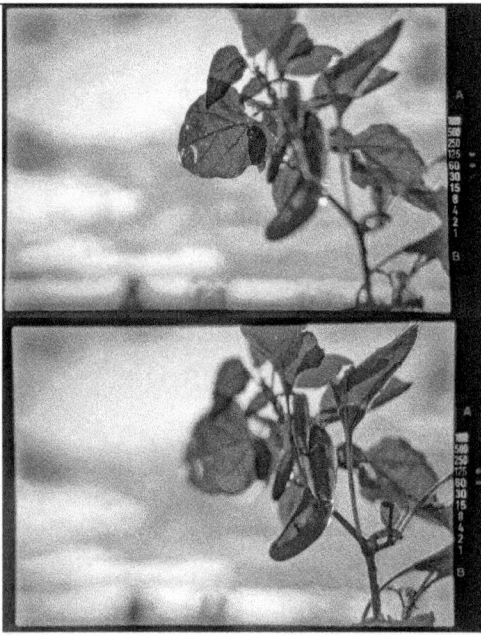

Figure 12: The viewfinder shows what is in focus as you adjust the lens.

Figure 12 provides photos taken through a Minolta X-370 viewfinder. In the top image, note that the veins on the jalapeno plant leaves are in crisp focus and that they align on the center split prism. In the bottom image, the nearest pepper is in focus but note how much different the leaf in the image center looks. These two photos show what proper focus in the center of the focusing screen versus missed focus look like. You can use this to obtain focus off-center by pointing the center of the focusing screen at an element of an image you would like to have be in focus, obtaining focus, and then recomposing the image to have that element off to the side.

4. Flash Basics

A camera flash lets you do many creative things with your Minolta X-370. Here are some statistics about your camera's flash capabilities. This chapter will explain what each means and provide tips to use a flash effectively.

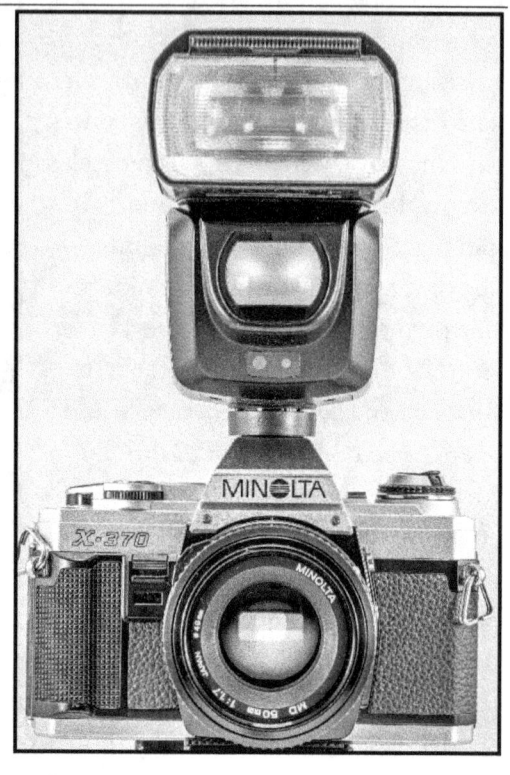

1- Hot shoe: Yes
2- PC port? No
3- Sync speed: 1/60th
4- Flash types: X only

Your camera includes a hot shoe for "X" (xenon) flashes. An X flash has a reusable bulb. If you can use the flash over and over, it will work properly on the camera. The hot shoe powers a standard flash unit.

The Minolta X-370 has a 1/60th of a second flash sync speed. That means that the camera's fastest shutter speed where a flash will work properly is 1/60th. The red color of the 60 on the shutter speed dial is a reminder not to go faster. You can go slower. The flash will work at any speed from 1/60th to a full second and bulb. In fact, with bulb, you can hold the shutter open for seconds or minutes and trigger a flash in your hand or with a remote exactly when you want to.

The reason that the flash sync speed is 1/60th is that's the fastest shutter speed at which the camera's two focal plane shutter curtains are both open and the entire film area is exposed to light. Shutter speeds are controlled by the shutter curtains. The first curtain opens and then, after the shutter speed period, the second closes. When you advance the film, both curtains reset.

At 1/60th, the first curtain opens, the whole film area is exposed to light for about 1/60th of a second, and then the second curtain closes. At 1/15th, the same is true but the whole film area is exposed to light for about 1/15th of a second. At faster shutter speeds, say 1/500th, the first curtain opens and then the second curtain follows quickly behind it. A slit between the curtains passes over the film and at no time is the entire film plane exposed to the light all at once. If you triggered a flash with your camera at 1/500th your image would be an illuminated strip off to the side of your photo. The camera's flash will trigger when the first curtain completes its travel and, at shutter speeds faster than 1/60th, the second curtain will be close behind it blocking much of the film.

Understanding the basics of your camera's mechanical flash operation, here are some flash-use tips for you:

1- An inexpensive flash with manual power controls is ideal for the X-370.

2- Humans are wired to see subjects lit from above as normal. Outside, our world is lit by the sun, inside by overhead lights. To our minds, lighting from above is flattering. Use your flash to replicate overhead lighting.

3- The worst possible place for a flash is in a camera's hot shoe with the flash output pointed at the subject. That arrangement leads to flat and waxy-looking subjects because the light reaches them in a flat burst and bounces back to the lens in a flat reflection.

Fortunately, some simple things can help obtain great flash results. A flash with a tilting (up and down) and swiveling (left and right), or fully articulating (both), output lets you use the hot shoe and bounce light off a ceiling or wall to mimic light our brains see as flattering. **Figure 13** depicts such a flash.

Using a flash is an art form itself and a lot of great photographers spend their careers learning to be adept at flash use. These basics should be enough to get you started, though.

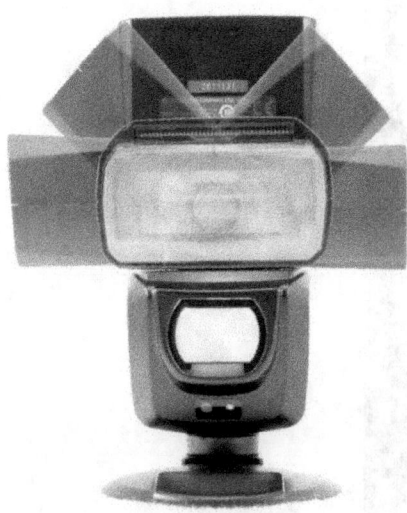

Figure 13: Articulating flashes help create flattering light.

5. Reading the Light Meter

Figure 14 shows the Minolta X-370's light meter display as seen through the viewfinder. The viewfinder provides a shutter speed scale, light-emitting diode (LED) indicator lights to the right of each shutter speed number, two triangles to indicate if the camera needs more or less light, and manual (M) and AUTO (A) indicators to let you know if your camera is set to a manual shutter speed or an automatic shutter speed (the latter of which is based on the aperture you select.) This mock-up of the viewfinder light meter display shows what the display would look like if every possible indicator could be illuminated at once.

Shooting in manual mode can cause incorrect exposures if the meter information isn't followed. **Figure 15** below shows different light meter readouts to help you understand what the light meter is indicating. Check each of the six examples and see if you can figure out what the light meter indicates. The paragraphs after Figure 15 will help you confirm if you're correct.

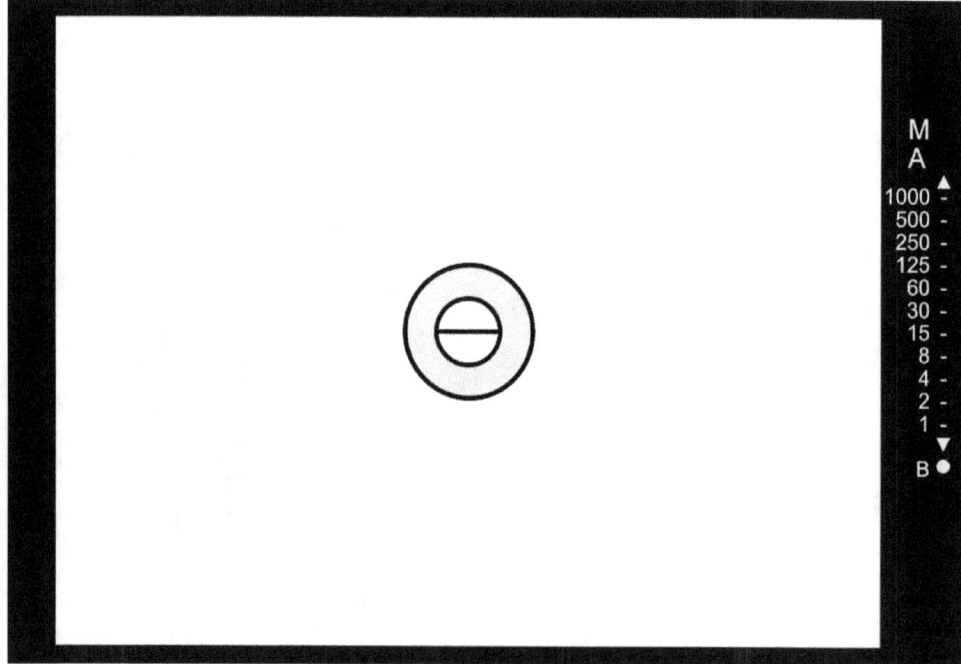

Figure 14: The light meter display is easily understood.

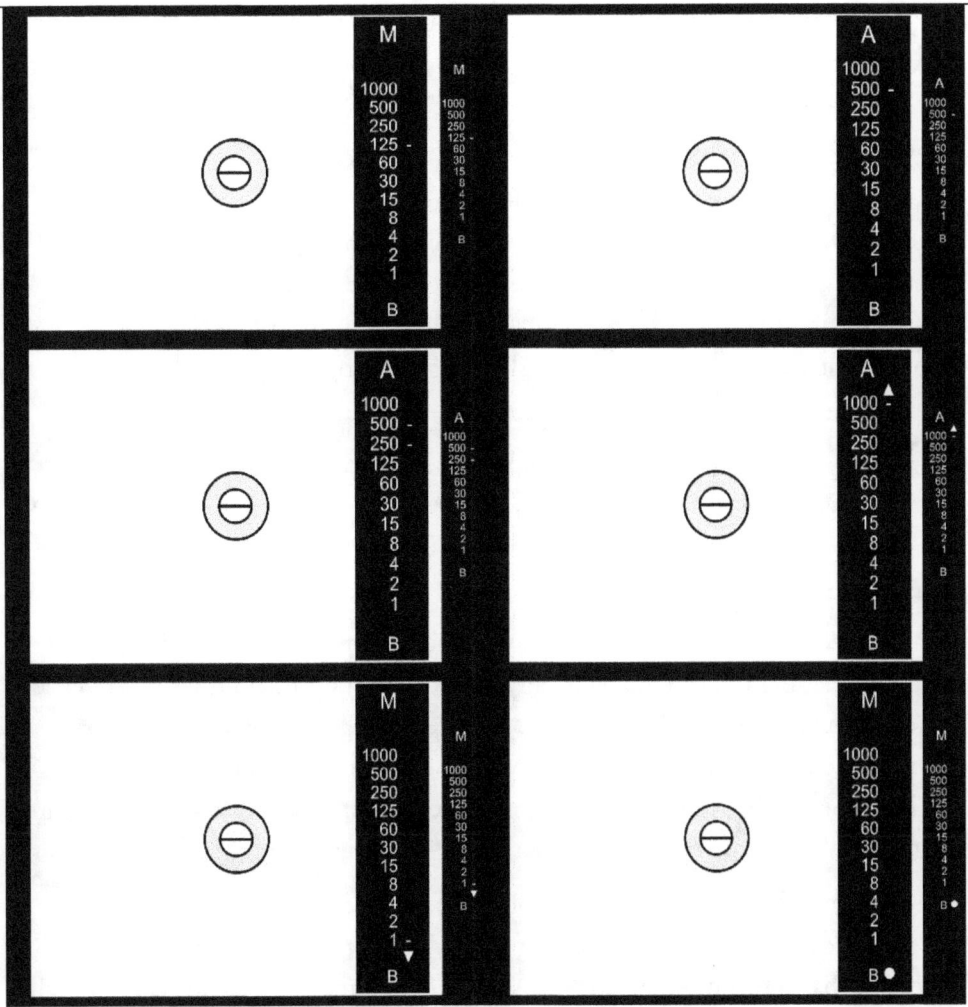

Figure 15: The light meter communicates exposure data.

The six scenarios above provide six different potential meter readouts. Based on what you know about the camera so far, try and explain each and then read below to find out if you were correct. Each meter display is enlarged for reading.

In the top left, the meter display shows manual shutter speed selection (the M at the top) and a blinking light is on next to the 125. This indicates that the camera is set to 1/125th of a second for the shutter speed and that the meter reading is correct. In a related scenario not shown above, if the 125 was blinking but the 60 were solid, the camera would be telling you that you need to adjust the shutter speed to 1/60th to obtain a proper exposure and that 1/125th is not a proper shutter speed for your film speed, available light, or aperture. You could also, in this latter scenario, adjust the aperture to obtain a proper exposure. Here is how to remember key information in manual exposure mode: A blinking light indicates your selected shutter speed, a solid light indicates the shutter speed you need based on your aperture, and the absence of a solid light means you've picked the correct shutter speed.

In the top right, the illuminated A indicates that the camera is set to AUTO mode and that it will select a shutter speed based on your selected aperture, film speed, and available light. In this readout, the camera has a solid light next to the 500, indicating that the camera will use a $1/500^{th}$ shutter speed. This will change if you adjust your aperture or the available light changes.

In the middle left, the camera indicates AUTO mode and the light by the 500 and 250 are both illuminated and solid. This is the camera's way of indicating that the shutter speed will be between those two speeds. Yes – in AUTO the X-370 can use shutter speeds between the marked speeds.

In the middle right, the "A" and the light beside the 1000 are illuminated. The red triangle is blinking. This indicates that the camera is in AUTO mode, that the light reaching the camera is too great, and that the camera does not have a fast enough shutter speed with the rest of the settings as they are to obtain a proper exposure. If you take a photo with the top triangle blinking, the photo will likely be too bright. To correct this, adjust the aperture to a smaller opening (larger number) or take the photo in a setting with less light if possible.

The bottom left shows a solid "M", blinking light next to the 1, and blinking triangle below. This indicates that the camera is set to manual shutter speed selection, that the shutter speed is at a full second, and there is not enough light for this exposure. That last point means that the photo will likely be too dark. This could simply be because the lens cap is on or it could be that the scene is a night photo. If the lens cap is on, simply remove it. For a night photo, the camera needs to be set in "B" mode for a shutter speed longer than one second.

The bottom right shows what the light meter displays when the camera is in bulb mode. The light next to the "B" is a different shape for easy recognition. Bulb mode means that the shutter will stay open as long as the shutter button is pressed down. If you recall the cable release discussion above, a locking cable release can allow the camera, in bulb mode, to take very-long exposures (think hours for a waterfall at night, for example.)

Key to obtaining a proper meter reading, you'll need to ensure that your camera's ASA is set to the film's ISO (this is done once when loading the film,

Chapter 3.2.) Then to adjust the meter needle you'll adjust the shutter speed (on the camera's controls, Chapter 2.1) and the aperture ring (on the lens, **Figure 16**.) Your lens' specific aperture will vary by lens design. On the lens shown below, the aperture range is f/1.7 to f/22. Other lenses have different ranges.

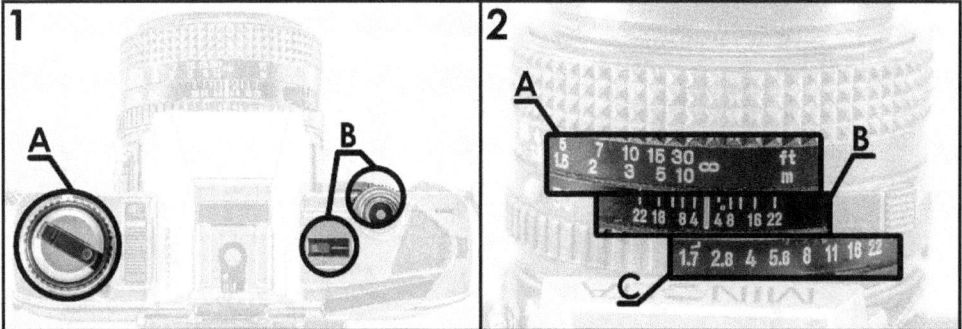

Figure 16: Exposure controls allow you to obtain a proper exposure.

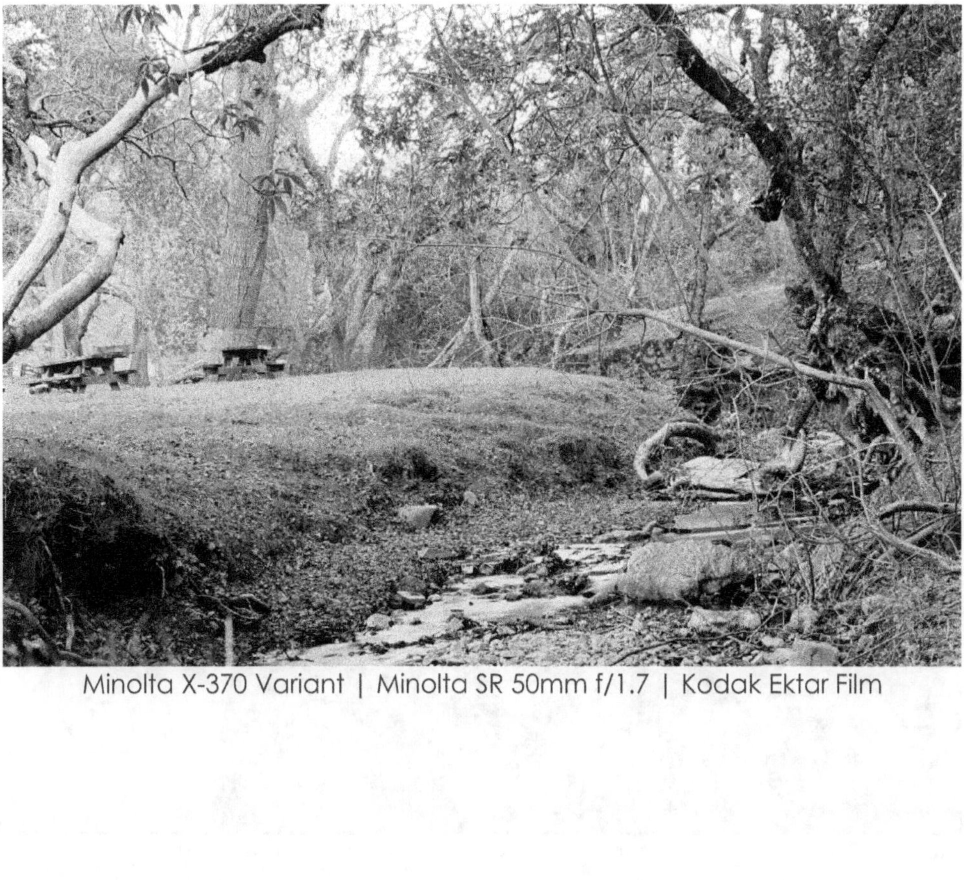

Minolta X-370 Variant | Minolta SR 50mm f/1.7 | Kodak Ektar Film

6. Take a Photo

Let's put everything we've just seen together to take a photo. By this point in the book, you should have a good grasp of basic operations. To take a photo, your camera should have a battery, film, and a lens. You'll hold the camera up to your eye and look through the viewfinder. Use the shutter speed dial and aperture ring to obtain a proper meter reading. Once your settings are dialed in, compose your image, focus, and press the shutter button. Afterward, advance the film. It's that easy. **Figure 17** illustrates the highly complex act of taking the photo. **Figure 18** shows the film advance lever's progression to advance the film.

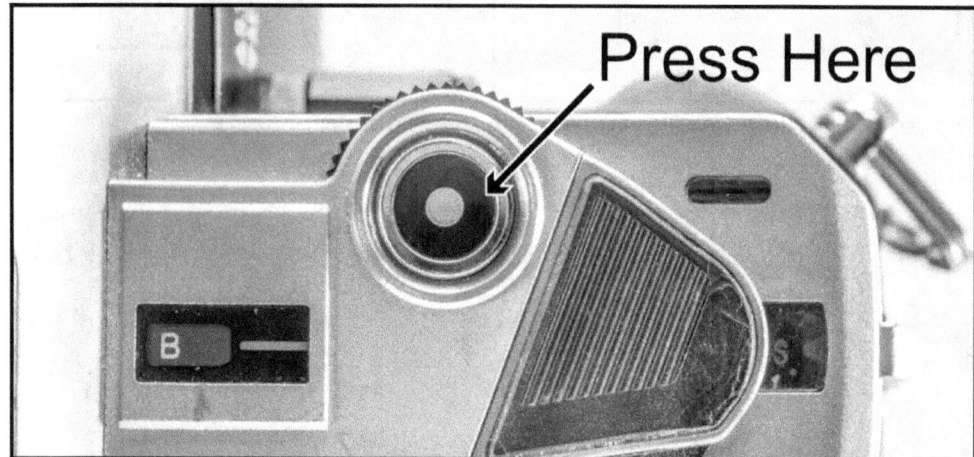

Figure 17: Set the shutter speed, aperture, and focus, then press.

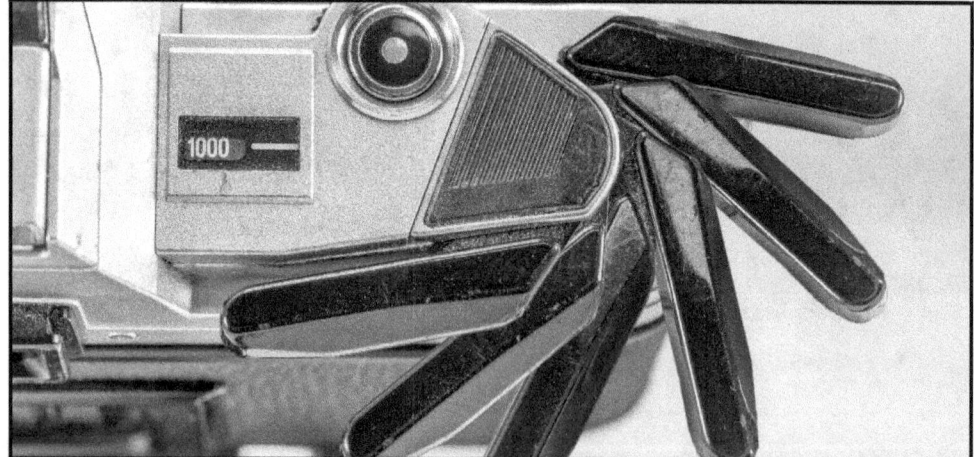

Figure 18: The advance lever moves the film and arms the shutter.

7. Tips for using the Minolta X-370

7.1. Using the Light Meter Effectively

As noted in the introduction, the camera includes a C-W TTL light meter. These meters, in general, use all the light from a scene, but bias the meter reading toward the light in the center of the scene, and determine a meter reading with little intrinsic accounting for different highlights and shadows within a scene. The Minolta X-370's meter is designed to attempt to make the scene a flat gray. This will work reliably in many conditions but exceptions, such as high-contrast scenes like snow or beaches, bright skies and dark foregrounds, and back-lit subjects can throw off the meter reading and ruin a photo.

When you find yourself in one of these scenes, the camera makes addressing this meter limitation easy. Here are some ways to combat meter misreadings.

Scenario 1: You're in the shade at a café with a bright beach, city, or another scene behind and you want to take a photo of the person you're with. The strong backlighting will cause them to be a silhouette while the scene behind is properly exposed. To counter this, point the camera at the ground in the shade and set your shutter speed and aperture, re-compose your photo, and take the photo without adjusting the settings. This will properly expose your subject at the cost of some of your background detail. Alternatively, you can take a meter reading from your subject with your camera about six inches from them. If you want to use AUTO mode for this function, then take your meter reading in either of the ways just described press the AEL button down and hold it until you take your photo. That will use the AEL button to lock exposure settings as lighting changes in the frame. You can also bracket your photos in this setting. To bracket your photos, take a reading of the scene as composed, another off the ground in the shade, and see what shutter speed difference exists. Take the first shot as described above and one or two more at shutter speeds between your selected speed and the as-metered scene reading.

For instance, let's say that you meter the shot as you want it and the camera says that at f/4 you need a $1/1{,}000^{th}$ shutter speed. Metering off the ground in the shade indicates that at f/4 a $1/125^{th}$ of a second shutter speed is correct. So try the shot at $1/125^{th}$, $1/250^{th}$, and $1/500^{th}$, all at f/4. One of those shots will be to your liking.

Scenario 2: You're at a beach or skiing in full sun. Snow illustrates this problem especially well because it's white and your camera's meter wants to make it gray; however, this same issue applies to beaches and other very-bright settings. Taking a photo as metered will make your images look muddy, which means low in contrast, and your snow and beach areas will look somewhat gray. Instead of taking the photo as metered, slow the shutter speed by one or two stops (clicks on the shutter dial.) If your camera says this scene needs $1/1,000^{th}$ of a second at f/8, try the shot at either $1/500^{th}$ or $1/250^{th}$. Alternatively, keep the $1/1,000^{th}$ shutter speed and try f/5.6 or f/4. This will let more light onto the film and help correct for the meter's functionality. And of course, you can also bracket in this situation.

7.2. How to take Double Exposures

The Minolta X-370 makes double-exposure photography fairly easily. Understanding the double-exposure image mechanical process is the more-complex element, so this instruction begins there.

1- Tighten the film rewind knob (by lifting the *lever* only, not the knob that releases the film door) and turning in the direction of the arrow until you feel resistance. This takes the slack out of the film, a needed step for the double exposure.
2- Take the first photo.
3- Hold the film rewind knob in your left fingers and press and *hold* the film rewind button on the camera's bottom while advancing the film. This re-arms the shutter without moving the film. If you don't hold the film rewind lever, the film may advance slightly and could ruin your double exposure. Attempting this without holding the film rewind button can damage the camera.
4- Take your second photo and advance the film normally.
5- As a good practice for double exposures, take a dead frame. This helps ensure that your carefully made double exposure does not overlap the next frame. Some cameras, when they begin to advance the film again after a double exposure, may not engage the advance gearing immediately. This can cause the double-exposure frame to only advance part way through the shutter area and lead to the next frame overlapping the double exposure. To take a dead frame, *put the lens cap on* the lens, set the shutter to the fastest shutter speed, and the aperture to the smallest

opening (highest aperture number.) Take a photo and then advance the film once more. This ensures that the film is advanced to unused media.

That process mastered, film is designed to record a certain number of photons and if a double-exposure frame receives two exposures worth of photons, then the double-exposure negative will be "thick", "dense", or "dark." These three words mean the same thing – the negative received too much light. In the darkroom, this leads to long print times and low contrast. In digitization, this leads to digital noise and low contrast. A good practice for double exposures is to cut the light for each exposure in half.

In AUTO mode, the Minolta X-370 makes this easy. Using the film speed dial, increase the speed one stop. For instance, if your camera has 200 ISO film loaded, set the film speed dial to 400. If you have 400 ISO film, then set it to 800. Recalling the discussion from the opening paragraph in Chapter 3.2, each time the film speed number doubles, the corresponding film speed needs half as much light. So for your double-exposure image, set the film speed dial to the number that is double the speed at which you're shooting your film and your camera will provide a correct exposure. Ensure that the film speed is reset to the correct setting when finished. That one step helps improve double-exposure image results.

In manual mode, the Minolta X-370 also makes this easy. With manual shooting, you can override the exposure settings (as illustrated in **Figure 19**) and the camera will do what you tell it to. After you obtain a proper exposure, simply change either the shutter speed (A) or aperture (B) to reduce the light by half. When you adjust the shutter speed by a click, you adjust it by one stop. Changing the shutter speed from $1/250^{th}$ to $1/500^{th}$ is a full stop that reduces the light passing through the shutter by half. Adjusting the shutter from $1/250^{th}$ to $1/125^{th}$ doubles the light passing through the shutter.

Aperture settings have the same effect. If you adjust your aperture from f/5.6 to f/8 – a full stop – you reduce the light passing through the aperture by half. Likewise, increasing it from f/5.6 to f/4 doubles the light passing through the aperture.

Assume you take a meter reading and a proper exposure is $1/250^{th}$ at f/5.6. For your double exposure you need to reduce the light reaching your film by half in each frame. You have two options with the Minolta X-370: use the shutter speed or use the aperture. Referencing the above paragraphs, you can set the shutter speed to 1/500th or the aperture to f/8 to reduce the light by half (don't make both adjustments.)

With your exposure level adjusted for the double exposure, you can follow the mechanical process described at the beginning of this chapter to complete the double exposure. If you're taking the double exposure in different settings with different lighting – for instance one indoors and one outdoors – then take a meter reading for each and simply cut the light reaching the film in each setting by half in the manner just described. Be sure to hold the film rewind button while you advance the film and then remember to take your dead frame.

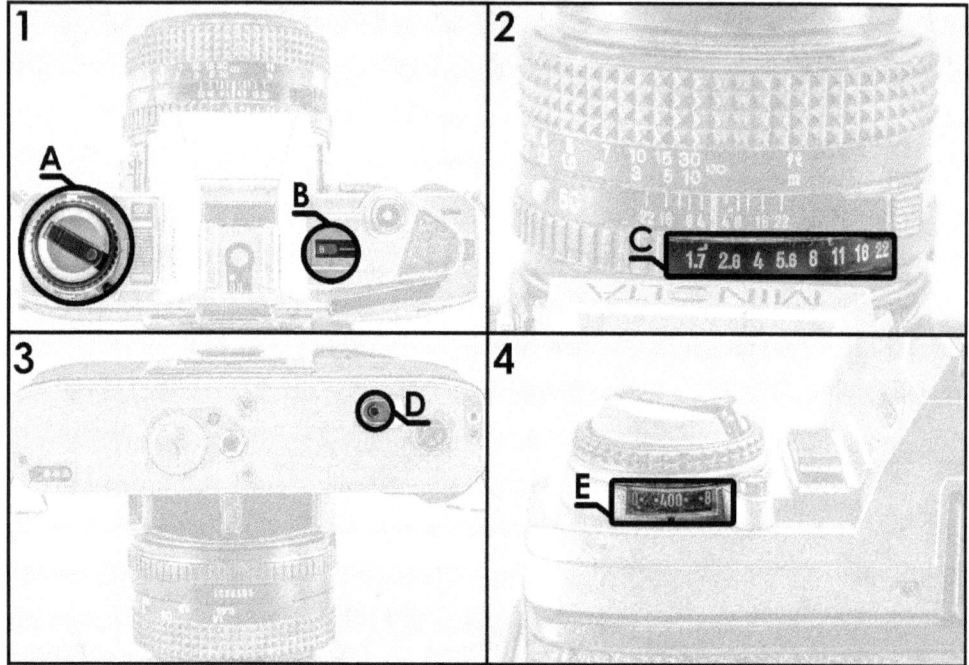

Figure 19: These controls help achieve proper double exposure results.

- A- In AUTO mode, simply adjust the film speed to compensate exposure settings during a double exposure.
- B- In manual shooting, adjust your shutter speed to compensate exposure settings for a double exposures.
- C- Alternative to shutter speed adjustment in manual mode, you can use your aperture instead.
- D- When you re-arm the shutter between photos, be sure to hold the film rewind button down and also hold the film rewind knob and lever.
- E- If you adjusted your film speed in AUTO mode, be sure to change it back.

7.3. General Care and Use

For basic tools to keep your camera clean, a bulb blower and natural brush (such as horsehair or camel hair) will do well to keep your lens elements, camera mirror, and focusing screen dust-free. Some lens cleaning tissues and spray will remove stuck-on lens dirt and grease. Cotton swabs and rubbing alcohol can clean your camera body. The David Hancock Channel has videos demonstrating how to properly clean lenses, cameras, and camera mirrors.

Some other basic things can help you keep your camera operating for the long term, too. Here are some good camera use practices:

1- Do not store the camera with the shutter ready to fire; always discharge it to release the tension on the springs and prevent shutter timing damage. Your camera is a mechanical device and arming the shutter puts the camera's mechanical pieces under tension. Leaving them under tension with an armed shutter can, with time, especially as these cameras age, cause springs to fatigue or break, which can affect camera shutter timing and operation.

2- Do not touch the shutter as this can brick your camera and cause it to need a professional repair.

3- Do not touch the mirror as your finger oils can tarnish the mirror. These are surface-coated with silver and tarnished mirrors can affect metering (your meter cells are in the camera's prism) and also affect focus accuracy. Also, be very gentle with the mirror if you need to clean it.

4- Do not leave your camera or lenses in your car because they can be a theft target and also be damaged by heat and cold. Cameras have lubricating grease and in heat, especially in a car, it can become very thin and flow to places it shouldn't be (such as lens apertures.) When it returns to proper viscosity, this can cause components to malfunction. Also, cold can cause those greases to break down and become gummy, which will affect operation.

5- Do not store your gear in a plastic bag or case because it increases the risk of lens coating and leather covering fungus. Plastic is moisture-permeable and moisture can get into plastic bags and cases. If you do store your camera in a plastic case, especially if you live in a humid location, invest in a rechargeable desiccant pack and keep it recharged when needed. That will do a lot to prevent your lenses from getting fungus.

6- Do not let your camera get wet. Your camera is not weather sealed and water in the camera will almost certainly ruin it.

Here is the most important thing I can tell you about your Minolta X-370: Your camera is a precision tool and should be handled with care and respect. As long as you take care of your camera, your camera will take care of you.

8. Known Problems

The Minolta X-370 is a reliable camera that has, by and large, lasted well. Honestly, given the market and price of these at release, they've held up remarkably and are cameras I'd easily and quickly recommend to people due to being reliable and low-maintenance. That said, there are some known problems to be mindful of:

1- **Capacitor Failure.** If your Minolta X-370 mirror is stuck mid-way between down and up or if the shutter won't fire (and there are good batteries installed) these are often, either singularly or together, indications that the camera's shutter capacitor has failed. The method for replacement is beyond this book's scope and many good videos and written resources exist online for how to perform this repair. If you have even basic soldering skills and a few minor tools, this is a repair that takes around ten minutes from when the soldering iron gets plugged in to when the camera's baseplate is re-attached. Here are the tools you will need:

   a. **Japanese Industrial Standard (JIS) screwdrivers.** Do not use Phillips head as they will damage the screws. JIS screwdrivers are easy to find online.

   b. **A soldering iron.** An inexpensive model will do. I used to perform this repair with a soldering iron I bought for around $10.

   c. **Some solder.** Just use the cheapest solder and don't use plumbing solder. I've never needed flux with this repair due to how minimal the soldering requirement is.

   d. **Solder wick.** You'll need to melt the existing solder and wick it away in order to complete this repair.

   e. **A replacement capacitor.** This camera needs one 220uf (microfarad) / 4-volt radial-lead electrolytic capacitor. One note to remember when you perform this repair, be sure to keep track of which terminal on the new and old capacitor is the positive as the new one has to go in correctly.

   f. **Wire snips.** You'll need to trim the new capacitor's leads to size.

2- **Stripped Advance Gearing.** This camera uses plastic advance gearing. Don't over-stress it and don't force film to advance if it doesn't want to. A stripped advance mechanism will manifest as an advance lever that feels floppy and doesn't do anything.

3- **Jammed Advance/Curtain Track Skip.** If your film advance lever feels jammed, firstly, don't force it as that's a great way to strip the advance gearing. Verify that the shutter has been fired and that the batteries are good. If the answer to those appears to be yes, or if the shutter button is non-responsive despite good batteries (this is especially true if the capacitor was just replaced) then the shutter curtains could have skipped their motion track. I've had a few of these cameras come through my hands with this issue and have had it fixed professionally some of the times. This is a significant and complex repair that should not be tried at home unless you're very familiar with camera repair.

4- **Light Seal Failure.** With age, the open-cell polyurethane foam used in light seals and for mirror bumpers (small pieces of foam inside the lens mount that protect the mirror when the shutter fires) can fail, turn to sticky goo, become dry and dusty, or break and fall out. When that happens, or even before, replacing them makes a lot of sense. The David Hancock Channel has a YouTube video on how to replace light seals with black cotton yarn. That video demonstrates this simple repair that you can almost certainly do yourself.

www.ingramcontent.com/pod-product-compliance
Lightning Source LLC
Chambersburg PA
CBHW070947220526
45471CB00007B/2932